BUILDING EQUITABLE EARLY LEARNING PROGRAMS

A Social-Justice Approach

By Ebonyse Mead, EdD, and Tameka Ardrey, PhD

www.gryphonhouse.com

Copyright

Bulk Purchase

Gryphon House books are available for special premiums and sales promotions as well as for fund-raising use. Special editions or book excerpts also can be created to specifications. For details, call 800.638.0928.

Disclaimer

Gryphon House, Inc., cannot be held responsible for damage, mishap, or injury incurred during the use of or because of activities in this book. Appropriate and reasonable caution and adult supervision of children involved in activities and corresponding to the age and capability of each child involved are recommended at all times. Do not leave children unattended at any time. Observe safety and caution at all times.

❧ TABLE OF CONTENTS ↷

INTRODUCTION 1

CHAPTER 1
The Manifestations of Institutional Racism. 10

CHAPTER 2
Understanding the Cultural Disconnect in
Early Childhood Education 18

CHAPTER 3
Supporting a Socially Just Early Childhood Workforce. 30

CHAPTER 4
Building Authentic Family Partnerships with Racially and
Ethnically Diverse Families 38

CHAPTER 5
Understanding Racially and Ethnically Diverse Learners 48

CHAPTER 6
Strengthening Teacher-Child Relationships with
Racially and Ethnically Diverse Learners 67

CHAPTER 7
Improving Instructional Practices with Racially and
Ethnically Diverse Learners 82

CHAPTER 8
Revising and Creating Equitable Policies and Practice 103

CHAPTER 9
Next Steps: Cultivating the Identity, Agency,
and Voice of Racially and Ethnically Diverse Learners 114

REFERENCES AND RECOMMENDED READING. 121

INDEX 137

Building Equitable Early Learning Programs: A Social-Justice Approach

INTRODUCTION

Who We Are

Ebonyse

I was born and raised in the North Lawndale community on the West Side of Chicago. Seeing many inequities in my neighborhood, I felt a deep sense of social responsibility to be a voice for those children and families often marginalized and excluded based on their zip codes. I started my career as a parent educator working with teen parents in Chicago public high schools. I have held numerous positions in which I advocated for the healthy development and well-being of families and children of color. In 2016, I was asked to sit on a workgroup to help develop a state's plan to address preschool suspension and expulsion. After reviewing the data that show Black preschoolers are 3.6 times more likely to be suspended than their white (U.S. Department of Education, 2016)* peers, I felt compelled to further address these inequities. Since that time, I have provided racial-equity training with a particular focus on examining structural barriers to educational equity, implicit racial bias, and culturally responsive instruction for the early childhood workforce. As a racial-equity consultant and early childhood professional, I am deeply committed to creating and promoting equitable and just programs in early childhood.

Tameka

My commitment to this work was born from an aha moment in a sociology of education course during my senior year of college. I remember being overwhelmed by feelings of discomfort and disbelief as my professor began to call into question the purpose of schooling and the implications of race for student outcomes. In particular, she highlighted the ways in which schools

---

* We lowercase *white* in this text but capitalize *Black*. For many people, *Black* reflects a shared identity and community. On the other hand, *white* is used more broadly to encompass a wide range of cultures and communities. Capitalizing the term *white* in the context of this book would risk following the lead of white supremacists.

were structured to prepare students for their roles in society by preparing white students to lead and students of color to serve. The content of the course challenged both who I was as an individual and what I believed about education. As an African American woman who had always been on the A/B honor roll and was only a semester away from graduation, I truly believed that schooling was a fair and equitable process independent of race or culture. However, all that changed after spending a few months volunteering in a third-grade classroom and witnessing inequitable and differential treatment of students simply based on the color of their skin. These inequities ranged from lower achievement expectations to harsher discipline practices for Black students. The culmination of this field experience marked the pivotal moment when I realized race and culture absolutely matter, and I vowed to do my part in advancing educational equity in early childhood education. From then on, I have done just that, both in and out of the classroom, serving in a variety of capacities, including as a teacher, administrator, and child-development specialist, and now as a college professor.

Together, we, the authors, have a total of thirty-eight years of experience in early childhood. We unite our experience as early childhood practitioners and higher-education faculty to write this book not only to help build an equity-minded early childhood workforce but also to help create early learning programs that are socially just.

The Changing Demographics of—and Cultural Disconnect in—Early Education

The demographics in the United States are increasingly more culturally and linguistically diverse. As our society continues to become more culturally and linguistically diverse, so do our early childhood classrooms and programs. Between 1994 and 2014, the percentage of children who are part of families who are recent immigrants, either first or second generation, increased by 45 percent, from 18 to 25 percent (Child Trends, 2018). In 2013, the National Center for Education Statistics reported that 50.3 percent of students in public school were children of color (Snyder, de Brey, and Dillow, 2016). The number of children of color in early learning programs has compelled early childhood professionals to rethink how we are educating and engaging with culturally diverse children and their families.

Research shows that a student's race, ethnicity, and cultural background—in conjunction with other variables including poverty, assessment practices, implicit bias, lack of professional development and training opportunities for teachers in culturally responsive instruction, and institutional racism—significantly influence many students' achievement (Harry and Klingner, 2006; Gilliam et al., 2016; Orosco and Klingner, 2010; Skiba et al., 2011). Students of color have unique learning styles and preferences that are rooted in their culture. For instance, African American students prefer a kinesthetic learning style that allows them to move around while learning. This kinesthetic learning style is related to the African American cultural value of *movement expressiveness* (Boykin, 1994), which is attributed to West African cultural values. When teachers lack knowledge of the unique learning styles of students of color, the students' behavior can be mislabeled or misread, thus leading to the student being reprimanded. To create equitable learning environments, we must address a cultural disconnect that exists between schools and homes. Many early childhood educators, specifically in the K–3 settings, are white, non-Hispanic, monolingual, and middle class (Gitanjali, Early, and Clifford, 2002; Banks and Banks, 2000). In addition, these educators often lack experience with and have limited exposure to children from racially and ethnically diverse backgrounds (Hollins and Guzman, 2005). They may not be comfortable discussing race (Gay and Howard, 2001).

Addressing the unique needs of racially and ethnically diverse students is imperative. It is vital that early learning programs be understanding, sensitive, and responsive to the diverse cultural needs, beliefs, and practices of their students and families. To create equitable learning environments, we need a paradigm shift. It is imperative that we prepare preservice teachers in culturally responsive anti-bias instruction; that educators, administrators, and policy makers adopt anti-racist perspectives; and that in-service teachers intentionally embed culturally relevant, sustaining pedagogies in their classrooms.

Creating equitable learning environments requires teachers, administrators, and support staff to have a deep understanding of the racial inequities that children of color experience. To do that, educators must deconstruct anti-Blackness and whiteness in educational settings. Deconstructing anti-Blackness means critically thinking about how anti-Blackness shows up in different aspects of the learning environment. For example, how does anti-Blackness show up in the classroom books? Are African American children or other children of color being portrayed in a stereotypical manner? Are they being depicted as the antagonist or the protagonist?

Are books about children of color positive, joyful, and uplifting, or are they negative and illustrate Black pain and suffering? *Deconstructing whiteness* means understanding how the American educational system was set up to perpetuate white advancement. This includes acknowledging that the assessments used and guidelines established for children's learning and development, such as the *Early Childhood Environment Rating Scales*, are often created from the perspective of a white worldview. This worldview is not inclusive or representative of the culturally and linguistically diverse children served in early learning programs.

Schools and programs need to establish a culture of equity that centers and prioritizes the voices of families of color and other families who have been traditionally marginalized and excluded from early childhood programs. Families of color must have shared power in decision-making to ensure their perspectives are considered. This requires an overall shift in beliefs and expectations toward the understanding that all students can be successful regardless of their racial, ethnic, or socioeconomic backgrounds and their gender, language, or ability. Education professionals must make a deep commitment to analyzing the root causes to address the inequities that exist within early learning environments. This book aims to provide guidance and support to help educators engage in these tasks.

What This Book Is About

Many books address culturally responsive instruction and anti-bias education in early childhood. These books serve as guides to help teachers create diverse and inclusive learning environments for all children. While these books are extremely valuable to the classroom teacher, not enough attention has been given to creating and sustaining equitable early learning programs in their entirely. In this book, we intentionally focus on the collective efforts of the administrator and the teacher to build equitable and inclusive learning environments by revising program policies, improving instructional practices, and building authentic family partnerships. We also dedicate a chapter to building the capacity of early childhood professionals to sustain equitable programs through communities of practice.

This book positions early childhood professionals to promote racial equity by addressing cultural disconnect, examining structural barriers to educational equity, and challenging their implicit biases. Given the vast racial disparities in education, such as the disproportionate rate at which Black preschool children are suspended, it is imperative that early childhood teachers create learning environments where children of color feel safe to learn in their own skin and where their families feel respected, valued, and empowered.

Chapter Descriptions

In chapter 1, we define institutional racism and explain how it creates systemic barriers based on race within our society. We also discuss the implications of historical trauma on people of color.

In chapter 2, we discuss the cultural disconnect in education and explore the ways in which meritocracy, implicit biases, and so-called color blindness undermine efforts to create equitable learning environments.

We emphasize transformative learning, self-reflection, and peer learning in chapter 3, as we explore the use of communities of practice as a strategy for helping teachers hone their skills in creating equitable learning environments.

Chapter 4 begins with a discussion of why traditional methods of family engagement may be insufficient for families of color. A discussion of the barriers to engaging with racially and ethnically diverse families follows. In this chapter, we define *culturally responsive family engagement* and why this approach to engaging families is preferred. This chapter highlights the ten "Diversity-Informed Tenets for Work with Infants, Children, and Families" (Irving B. Harris Foundation, n.d.) and how these tenets can apply to effectively engaging racially and ethnically diverse families.

Chapter 5 draws the reader's attention to the importance of understanding children in the context of their cultures and highlights the ways culture influences the learning styles of racially and ethnically diverse students.

Chapter 6 focuses on the transformative power of meaningful relationships between teachers and students and how to intentionally use these relationships to maximize learning and development.

In chapter 7, we provide a blueprint for effectively implementing culturally sustaining instructional practices that meet the developmental needs of racially and ethnically diverse students.

Using the critical issue of discipline disparities in early childhood education, chapter 8 highlights the importance of examining program practices and policies for potential biases that may negatively impact ethnically diverse students.

We discuss the importance of talking about race with young children in developmentally appropriate ways in chapter 9. The chapter offers concrete strategies teachers can employ for honest and open dialogues with young children concerning race and culture. We share a list of resources, including videos, websites, and books, to help teachers have authentic, age-appropriate conversations. We also offer a list of references and recommended reading to help you develop and deepen your understanding of culturally responsive and equitable learning environments, connecting with and building relationships with families, and supporting all the children you teach.

Our Invitation to You

Young children come into the classroom with their own funds of knowledge and unique needs. At times, caring for and educating young children may feel overwhelming because these children have so many varying needs. Teachers of young children may feel as if they have multiple roles, including social worker or therapist, outside of educating children. As early childhood professionals, we see you and applaud your efforts to provide the best learning experiences for our youngest children. We fully understand the challenges and rewards of educating young children. We also acknowledge that not all teachers have been adequately prepared to care for and educate culturally and linguistically diverse children. This book is a valuable tool to assist teachers and administrators in creating equitable learning environments that are culturally responsive and grounded in building authentic relationships with children and families and within the profession.

Authentic relationships provide an opportunity for us to be genuine and vulnerable within our communication and interactions. This vulnerability is what allows us to challenge our own biases, acknowledge the systemic barriers that have traditionally failed children of color and pathologized the interactions that families of color have with schools. When this vulnerability occurs, we are open to listening, learning, and acting in ways that foster equity and inclusion. We are preparing children to be high-functioning global citizens; therefore, we have a responsibility to ensure children have the best learning experiences regardless of their cultural, linguistic, or socioeconomic backgrounds.

As you read the text, we invite you to think about your instructional practices and the overall environment of your program. How might this book help you strengthen your current instructional practices and change them to be more culturally responsive? In what ways can your program better serve culturally and linguistically diverse children and families? How might this book improve your relationships with culturally diverse families? How might you challenge and support your colleagues to be more equity minded? In each chapter, we offer reflection questions for you to consider.

Keep in mind: Equity is not a destination. It is a continuous journey of learning and unlearning. You are not alone; this book serves to guide you on your journey. Enjoy!

GLOSSARY OF TERMS

As we have conversations about race and equity, it is incredibly important that we have shared definitions of the terms used to discuss race and equity so we all can be on the same page in our understanding.

Acculturation: refers to those individuals or groups who have developed a balance between their traditional culture and the majority culture (Schvaneveldt, 2022).

Anti-Blackness: is a form of racism that dehumanizes (devalues) Black people. It involves prejudice, stereotypes, discrimination, oppressions, attitudes, and beliefs about Black people that are rooted in colonization and slavery.

Assimilate: refers to individuals who have adopted the majority culture's values and retain little to no cultural traditions unique to their original culture (Schvaneveldt, 2022).

Critical race theory: involves studying and transforming the relationships among race, racism, and power relations. It is an alternative conceptualization of diversity and social hierarchy (Delgado and Stefancic, 2012).

Culture: refers to the norms, values, practices, patterns of communication, language, laws, customs, and meanings shared by a group of people located in a given time and place (Sensoy and DiAngelo, 2017).

Ethnicity: is the fact or state of belonging to a social group that has a common national or cultural tradition (DeGruy, 2009).

Historical trauma: is a form of collective complex trauma that impacts entire communities and is transmitted across generations (Statman-Weil, 2020).

Implicit bias: refers to the attitudes or stereotypes that affect our understanding, actions, and decisions in an unconscious manner (Staats, 2015).

Institutional racism: refers to the policies and practices, intentional or unintentional, that produce cumulative race-based inequities (Boutte, Lopez-Robertson, and Powers-Costello, 2011).

Microaggressions: are the everyday slights and insults that minoritized people endure and dominant people don't notice or concern themselves with (Sensoy and DiAngelo, 2017).

People of color: is "the term used to describe people who are racialized based on phenotypical features" (Sensoy and DiAngelo, 2017). The term *people of color* can be useful when describing similar experiences of racial discrimination and suffering experienced by racialized people. However, the term is also problematic, as it does not give space to the unique experiences of racial discrimination, injustices, and biases experienced by different racial and ethnic groups. The term often lumps all racialized people's experiences together and does not give way to the necessary investigation and injury of each group to fully understand their unique experience.

Post-traumatic slave syndrome: is a condition that exists as a consequence of multigenerational oppression of Africans and their descendants' following centuries of chattel slavery as well as the continued experiences of oppression and institutional racism (DeGruy, 2009).

Prejudice: learned presuppositions about members of social groups to which we don't belong (Sensoy and DiAngelo, 2017)

Race: is the classification of a group of people sharing the same culture, history, language, and other cultural characteristics. It also refers to a group or set of people with common features, for example, skin color, hair texture, and eye shape or color (DeGruy, 2009).

Racial equity: is a process of eliminating racial disparities and improving outcomes for everyone. It is the intentional and continual practice of changing policies, practices, systems, and structures by prioritizing measurable change in the lives of people of color (Race Forward, n.d.).

Racism: refers to white racial and cultural prejudice and discrimination, supported by institutional power and authority, used to the advantage of white people and to the disadvantage of people of color. Racism encompasses economic, political, social, and institutional actions and beliefs that systematize and perpetuate an unequal distribution of privileges, resources, and power between white people and people of color (Sensoy and DiAngelo, 2017).

Socialization: refers to our systematic training into the norms of our culture (Sensoy and DiAngelo, 2017).

Stereotype threat: refers to a concern that a person will be evaluated negatively due to stereotypes about their racial group; that concern causes the person to perform poorly, thereby reinforcing the stereotype (Sensoy and DiAngelo, 2017).

Whiteness: refers to the specific dimensions of racism that elevate white people over all peoples of color (Sensoy and DiAngelo, 2017).

CHAPTER 1

The Manifestations of Institutional Racism

How Institutional Racism Functions

Institutional racism is deeply embedded within normative American society. Institutional racism refers to the discriminatory policies, practices, and unequal opportunities—both intentional and unintentional—that produce cumulative race-based inequities (Boutte, Lopez-Robertson, and Powers-Costello, 2011). Racism has permeated many American institutions, including education, health care, and the criminal justice system, and has been upheld both historically (for example, through "separate but equal" policies) and currently (for example, through mass incarceration) through laws and racist beliefs and attitudes. The inequities that exist within American institutions can be attributed to institutional racism.

Understanding how institutional racism operates is imperative for understanding the inequities within American society. Golash-Boza (2016) argues that racist beliefs produce racist institutions, and, in turn, racist institutions reinforce racist beliefs that impact practices, policies, and laws and perpetuate racial discrimination and bias. Throughout American history, the myth of white superiority suggests that white people are superior and all other races are inferior. White superiority functions as a cultural narrative and norm within American society. This cultural norm serves as the justification for white dominance, resulting in inequitable outcomes that privilege white individuals and disprivilege people of color. There are numerous racial inequities that have grave implications for the lives of African Americans and other people of color. In the next section, we will look at inequities in housing, education, poverty, health care, and incarceration that are rooted in institutional racism.

Housing

Before the 1968 Fair Housing Act, Black Americans and other people of color were prohibited from living in certain areas, even if they could afford to purchase a home there. The federal government, specifically the Federal Housing Administration and the Home Owners' Loan Corporation, played a significant role in racial housing segregation. Through policies such as *redlining*—the color-coding of maps that displayed the safest and riskiest neighborhoods in America—African Americans were prohibited from residing in certain neighborhoods. The safest neighborhoods were outlined in green, and the riskiest neighborhoods—typically where African Americans and other people of color resided—were highlighted in red (Rothstein, 2017). Another practice instrumental in racial housing segregation was the inclusion of restrictive covenants in home deeds. *Restrictive covenants* were clauses in home deeds that prevented the sale or future resale of homes to African Americans. With these practices in place, African Americans, and even African American veterans, found it extremely difficult to qualify for home loans.

The Federal Housing Administration and the Veterans Administration mortgage programs primarily served white applicants (Rothstein, 2017). These practices excluded African Americans and other people of color from accumulating wealth through ownership. The implications of these racist policies and practices contribute to the inequities in housing and wealth between African American and white Americans today—referred to as the wealth gap.

Education

Racial housing segregation and school segregation are uniquely connected. To keep African American families from living in white neighborhoods, districts would place the only school that served African American students in designated African American neighborhoods and would provide no transportation for African American students who resided elsewhere (Rothstein, 2017). African American families were forced to live in those neighborhoods so their children could have access to education.

Brown v. Board of Education of Topeka (1954) (often referred to as *Brown v. Board*) was supposed to be the great equalizer that eliminated the racial inequalities within America. Education has always been seen as a pathway to social mobility, especially for African Americans. However, more than sixty years after *Brown v. Board*, children of color and African American children in particular are attending public schools that are more segregated by race and class today than they were prior to the landmark court decision. The racial inequities within American schools are commonplace. African American children and other children of color are more likely to be identified as having special needs and are less likely to be recommended for gifted and talented programs (York, 2016). African American preschool children are 3.6 times more likely to be suspended more than once compared to their white peers (U.S. Department of Education, 2016). Unfortunately, the pattern of suspension continues as African American children matriculate through school. According to the U.S. GAO (2020), disparities in school discipline are prevalent, as African American students, boys, and students with disabilities are disproportionately disciplined through practices such as suspension or expulsion. Access to high-quality early childhood programs is another inequity that disadvantages children of color. Because African American and Latine children are less likely to attend high-quality early childhood programs (York, 2016), they are less likely to be prepared for kindergarten.

Efforts to address racial inequities in education have not been effective. Despite the passage of the Elementary and Secondary Education Act of 1965 and the intentions of the No Child Left Behind Act of 2001, racial inequities for African American children and other children of color continue to be widespread. African American children are more likely to attend schools that are poorly resourced, have less qualified teachers, and offer lower quality instruction, outdated textbooks, and inadequate facilities (Milner, 2006; Tileston, 2010). Sadly, the promise of *Brown v. Board* has yet to be realized.

Poverty

Racial discrimination in housing and employment practices such as hiring, pay, promotion, and retention is connected to the disproportionate rates at which families and children of color experience poverty. In a 2015 study, the Pew Research Center found that white men out-earned African American and Latine men and women (Patten, 2016). They also found that Asian and white women were paid eighteen and seventeen dollars, respectively, less than white men. African American and Latina women earned thirteen and twelve dollars, respectively, less than white men. However, Asian and white women earned more than African American and Latino men, who earned an average of fourteen to fifteen dollars an hour. Similarly, there are disparities in housing. According to the National Low-Income Housing

Coalition (2019), 20 percent of African American households, 18 percent of Native American households, and 16 percent of Hispanic households are extremely low-income renters; whereas, 6 percent of white households are extremely low-income renters.

Disparities in homeownership rates are also prevalent. USAFacts.org (2020) reported that, in 2019, homeownership rates among white families were 73.3 percent compared to 42.1 percent among African Americans. Rates were 47.5 percent for Latine families, 50.8 percent among American Indians or Alaska Natives, and 57.7 percent among Asian or Pacific Islander Americans. Pervasive discriminatory housing policies contribute to the wealth gap between white people and people of color. According to USAFacts.org (2020), in 2019 white households owned 85.5 percent of wealth, African American households owned 4.2 percent, and Hispanic households owned 3.1 percent.

Race and poverty are inextricably linked. Systemic barriers in housing and employment significantly account for the disproportionate rates of poverty among families of color. According to the Children's Defense Fund (2021), 71 percent of children in poverty are children of color. A recent study by the Pew Research Center found African American and Hispanic children are overrepresented in poverty (Pew Research Center, 2020). About 38 percent of African American children are still living below the poverty line, and Hispanic children represent 41 percent of all impoverished Hispanics.

The association between poverty and education has been well documented. Young children living in poverty are less likely to attend preschool than children from middle-income or higher-income families (Bredekamp, 2019). In fact, only 18 percent of low-income children are enrolled in high-quality preschool programs (Nores and Barnett, 2014). Further, "Children from low-income families often do not receive the stimulation and do not learn the social skills required to prepare them for school" (Ferguson, Bovaird, and Mueller, 2007). Therefore, children of color and low-income children enter school already behind their more affluent peers. Additionally, the stress related to poverty can adversely impact a child's ability to learn. Children living in poverty may have less access to healthy and nutritious foods and may live in inadequate housing. These factors can severely impact a child's academic performance (Grant and Ray, 2013). It's difficult for a child to concentrate when they are hungry or do not know where they will be sleeping for the night.

Health Care

Inequities within the American health-care system that disproportionately impact African American people and other people of color are plentiful. People of color are more likely to be uninsured in America, thus leading to uneven access to health-care services and poor overall health outcomes. Systemic barriers based on race continue to impact the well-being of African American children and other children of color. For example, according to the 2019, National Vital Statistics Report, the infant mortality rate for infants of non-Hispanic Black women was more than twice as high as that for infants of non-Hispanic white women, non-Hispanic Asian women, and Hispanic women (Ely and Driscoll, 2021).

Other disparities exist in medical care and dental hygiene. According to a study published in *JAMA Network Open* (Marin et al., 2021), African American and Latine children entering emergency rooms are less likely than white children to receive X-rays, CT scans, and other diagnostic imaging tests. Disparities are also found in dental hygiene for young children of color. Data analyzed by the Pew Charitable Trusts (Corr and Wenderoff, 2022) found that the frequency of treated and untreated tooth decay among American Indian, Alaska Native, Native Hawaiian, Hispanic, and African American third graders is considerably higher than that found in their white peers. These pervasive disparities can impact the overall physical well-being for children of color, thus affecting their ability to be successful in school.

Mass Incarceration

The Netflix documentary *13th*, directed by Ava DuVernay (2016), illustrates the vast disparities in incarceration rates between people of color, especially Latino and African American men, and white men. Findings from the Department of Justice (Bronson and Carson, 2019) suggest that one of every three African American males born today can expect to go to prison in his lifetime, as can one of every six Latino males, compared to one in seventeen white males. A study conducted by the National Registry of Exonerations (Gross, Possley, and Stephens, 2017) found that African American adults are seven times more likely to be imprisoned than white Americans. In 2017, Black males ages eighteen and nineteen were roughly twelve times more likely than white males of the same ages to be incarcerated (Bronson and Carson, 2019).

Racism is inherent within the criminal justice system. After slavery was abolished in the United States, Black codes and vagrancy laws were established as a form of racial control; these measures severely restricted the new freedom of African Americans. Many Southern white landowners still needed a cheap labor force after slavery ended. Black codes and vagrancy laws allowed Southern white Americans to maintain a cheap labor workforce (Alexander, 2012). For example, many states required African Americans to sign yearly labor contracts. Failure to sign those contracts could result in a fine or prison. Similarly, vagrancy laws made it illegal for people to be jobless or homeless. These laws prohibited people from wandering and were instituted as many newly freed African Americans searched for work and for their family members who had been sold during slavery. If African Americans could not provide proof of employment, they were often arrested and sent to prison. These blatantly racist policies are the origins of mass incarceration in the United States.

The incarceration of a parent or loved one has significant social and emotional impacts on the development of young children. Incarceration of a parent or primary caregiver can impact the family's financial well-being and lead to or worsen housing instability. The stress of worrying about a family member's well-being can affect the mental health of children and other family members. These experiences can lead to or exacerbate anxiety, depression, and other mental illness and behaviors in young children and their families.

Understanding the Role of Historical Trauma

Institutional racism and historical trauma (also referred to as *intergenerational trauma*) are uniquely connected. Communities impacted by intergenerational trauma in the United States include members of the African American community who survived slavery and Jim Crow laws and their descendants, Indigenous peoples who survived genocide and displacement and their descendants, and those who survived the Holocaust and their descendants.

Historical trauma is a form of collective complex trauma that impacts entire communities and is transmitted across generations (Statman-Weil, 2020). Because historical trauma exists on the individual, interpersonal, and community levels, race-based traumatic stress can affect the functioning and well-being of communities. For example, the impact of remembering and dealing with the denigration of one's community and the ongoing effects of stress due to societal racism (Hemmings and Evans, 2018) cause mental and physical stress to groups that experience historical trauma. Statman-Weil (2020) states that historical trauma can be seen in the descendants of trauma survivors whose communities have suffered major trauma or abuses.

Historical trauma impacts the physical, psychological, and social health of individuals and communities. The connection between racism and trauma has been well documented. For example, Indigenous peoples of the Americas experience high rates of substance abuse due to the ongoing devastating effects of colonialism and mass genocide (Nutton and Fast, 2015). Research also concludes that Indigenous peoples are likely to have increased rates of mental illness. Janzen and colleagues (2017) found an association between racism and depression among Indigenous people. Similarly, African Americans also experience poor health and social outcomes. According to the Harvard T. H. Chan School of Public Health (2016), African Americans have higher rates of diabetes, hypertension, and heart disease than white Americans, demonstrating the higher likelihood of poor health outcomes. The negative mental and physical health outcomes experienced by Indigenous peoples and African Americans can be attributed to the devastating and compounding effects of historical trauma. Dr. Joy DeGruy (2017) uses the term *post-traumatic slave syndrome* (PTSS) to explain the continuous harm of racial oppression and discrimination. PTSS is defined as the prolonged exposure to a multitude of mental, emotional, and physical injuries coupled with ongoing discriminatory and oppressive practices.

There is currently a growing movement to address trauma in early childhood. While focusing on individual traumas that young children may experience is important, there also must be a focus on historical and racial trauma. The role of historical and racial trauma affects not only children's development but also their outcomes. The legacies of slavery, the remnants of Jim Crow, and the atrocities of mass genocide and displacement are still present in many Indigenous and African American communities. Being aware of the effects of intergenerational trauma on children's learning and development allows educators, administrators, and other staff to better understand the cultural backgrounds and some of the behaviors of the children and families with whom they work and to provide supportive practices that are culturally responsive and trauma informed.

Institutional racism is upheld in part by the unfair policies and discriminatory practices that routinely produce inequitable outcomes for people of color. The inequities in housing, education, poverty, health care, and mass incarceration are all examples of institutional racism. Acknowledging the significance of institutional racism is vital to addressing the racial inequities within education and in early childhood education in particular. Educators and administrators must conduct a thorough examination of the policies and practices, such as suspension policies, that maintain inequitable outcomes. Additionally, challenging and interrupting the racist beliefs that influence discriminatory policies and practices is a necessary requirement for dismantling institutional racism within education.

Implicit racial biases can influence teachers' and administrators' interactions and responses to students of color. Students of color, in particular African American boys, have often been accused of being aggressive, lacking motivation, being uninterested in learning, and not being as smart as their white peers (Lewis and Diamond, 2015; Tileston, 2010; Kunjufu, 2002). These racialized stereotypes produce inequitable outcomes for children of color. Early childhood educators need adequate skills, ongoing training and development in culturally responsive anti-bias practices, and a nuanced understanding of the prevalence and role of racism within education. A paradigm shift in the way teachers teach, support, and engage with students of color is necessary to support the unique learning needs of culturally and linguistically diverse learners. In the next chapter, we will take a closer look at the cultural disconnect within education.

REFLECTING ON INSTITUTIONAL RACISM

✦ Do you think institutional racism has affected your teaching practices? Why or why not?

✦ Considering what you have read about institutional racism, in what ways can you challenge institutional racism in early childhood education?

✦ How can you create equitable educational opportunities for children and families from groups who have been historically marginalized?

Understanding the Cultural Disconnect in Early Childhood Education

The field of early childhood focuses on educational programs that serve children from birth to age eight and their families. Learning through play and family engagement are integral components of early childhood education. Research has shown that positive early experiences can set young children on a healthy trajectory for school and later life. One could argue then that early childhood experiences can often give young children a jump start in life. In fact, there are several early childhood programs and initiatives, such as Head Start, that adhere to this concept. President Lyndon B. Johnson signed the Economic Opportunity Act in 1964, creating various programs, including Head Start, with the intent to fight against poverty in the United States. Yet while Head Start and other early childhood programs strive to create high-quality early learning experiences for all young children, many children of color experience disparate outcomes.

For example, culturally and linguistically diverse children are overrepresented in special education (Counts, Katsiyannis, and Whitford, 2018; Sullivan, 2011; O'Connor and DeLuca-Fernandez, 2006), and African American children are disproportionately suspended and expelled even in preschool (Losen and Skiba, 2010; Gilliam et al., 2016; U.S. Department of Education, 2014). Recent statistics suggest African American children make up only 19 percent of preschool enrollment but represent 47 percent of preschoolers suspended one or more times (U.S. Department of Education, 2014).

As educators caring for the well-being of all young children, we must ask ourselves what is driving the disparities in education for young children.

Concepts such as color blindness, meritocracy, and implicit racial bias contribute to the cultural disconnect in American schools and unintentionally perpetuate racial inequities. There is often a cultural disconnect between teacher-education programs, early childhood teachers, and the culturally diverse children they serve.

The challenge is that, according to a report from National Center for Education Statistics (2013), 82 percent of teachers in American public schools are European American. Additionally, 40 percent of schools do not have a single teacher of color. White teachers who are ill-prepared to engage with and educate children of color perpetuate a situation that threatens children's academic achievement. Inadequate preparation can create a cultural gap between teachers and students (Gay, 2010; Ladson-Billings, 2009). Derman-Sparks, LeeKeenan, and Nimmo (2015) assert that many early childhood programs are rooted in white European-American culture, thus influencing curriculum, instruction, policies, practices, and the overall learning environment. As a result, the cultural and linguistic characteristics of diverse learners are often not organically incorporated into the learning environment (Orosco and Klingner, 2010). Addressing this cultural disconnect is paramount to ensuring that all children have positive educational outcomes.

Many educators teaching in urban schools are not trained to deal with the unique learning styles and needs of African American students or the issues they face daily in their community. Kunjufu (2002) argues that teacher-education programs have not adequately prepared teachers to teach in urban areas. The author asserts that many white teachers working in urban schools have never taken a course in Black studies, lack knowledge of Black history and culture, and are unfamiliar with the unique learning styles of African American students. How can we expect teachers to educate children of color when they lack knowledge of the children's cultural history and heritage? This chapter will discuss the different factors that contribute to racial inequities in early childhood education.

The "Color-Blind" Approach and Meritocracy

Many early childhood teachers are trained to adopt a color-blind ideology that aims to treat all children equally and to ignore or dismiss racial differences (Boutte, Lopez-Robinson, and Powers-Costello, 2011; Meece and Wingate, 2009). Such teachers may express statements such as, "I don't care if children are African American, white, or green with polka dots. I treat all children the same" (Boutte, Lopez-Robinson, and Powers-Costello, 2011), or "Kids are kids" (Meece and Wingate). While the intent of a color-blind approach is to treat children equally and fairly, this approach ignores the issues of race, institutional biases, discrimination, and prejudices in education (Wardle, 2007; York, 2016).

Color-blind ideology grew out of the civil rights movement. African Americans civil rights activists such as Martin Luther King, Jr., Prathia Hall, A. Philip Randolph, and Fannie Lou Hamer fought diligently to end racial discrimination, housing segregation, educational inequality, and other race-based injustices in the United States. In Dr. King's famous "I Have a Dream" speech, he states, "I have a dream that my four little children will one day live in a nation where they will not be judged by the color of their skin but by the content of their character" (King, 1963). This idea of not being judged by the color of one's skin was seen as a way to promote race-neutral policies and racial equality.

Color blindness suggests the best way to address and end racial discrimination is by treating individuals as equally as possible, without regard to race, culture, or ethnicity (Schofield, 2010). However, sociologist Eduardo Bonilla-Silva (2018) argues that this ideology is actually a form of racism that erases the current, lived, and systemic oppression and institutional discrimination of people of color. A color-blind ideology suggests that there is no racial hierarchy in our society and that the prevalence of race is insignificant. Contrary to this idea, Bonilla-Silva argues that color-blind racism rationalizes racial inequality using nonracial language such as *meritocracy*—the idea that if a person works hard, they can achieve whatever they want. This will be discussed further later in the chapter.

For the past thirty years, multicultural education has been seen as the path by which to address inequalities in education. While multicultural education is multifaceted, at its core is the idea to reject racial discrimination and promote equality in education. That said, many white educators have adopted a color-blind approach to cultural diversity. They believe that teaching children how they are the same rather than acknowledging and celebrating their differences will cause less prejudice to occur (Derman-Sparks and Edwards, 2010; Meece and Wingate, 2010). Yet the reality is that applying a color-blind approach in early childhood programs is counterproductive to achieving racial equity because it fails to highlight the unique histories, cultures, values, and experiences of children of color (Boutte, Lopez-Robertson, and Powers-Costello, 2011; Schofield, 2007). A color-blind approach, paradoxically, is often seen as a best practice in education when many of the inequities in society are based on the color of one's skin.

Unfortunately, color-blind ideology prevents educators from thinking critically about race and can ultimately lead to more biases. Minami and Ovando (2004) state that teachers often view children from other cultures through a deficit lens. The influence of culture on students' achievement in relation to racial inequalities in schools is a continued topic of discussion within education. One theory that has been explored is the *cultural deprivation theory*, which has been widely used in the field of sociology to analyze the underachievement of African American students. This theory takes a deficit perspective and places blame on African American children and families for the students' underachievement. The cultural deprivation theory posits that African Americans have deep-seated fundamental problems within their community that have implications for students' negative attitudes toward education and their ability to succeed (Friedman, 1967). For example, the cultural deprivation theory will blame poverty, inadequate health care and housing, lack of healthy and nutritious food, and mass incarceration of African Americans instead of analyzing the long-standing institutional barriers that oppress and discriminate against African Americans.

The theory is problematic because it ignores the barriers created by institutional racism that have historically prohibited African American children from obtaining an equitable education in America. Sullivan (2016) argues that teachers viewing African American children through a deficit lens often leads to *pathologizing* young children—treating them as psychologically abnormal or unhealthy. Allen, Scott, and Lewis (2013) argue that the beliefs and attitudes teachers hold about their students' abilities, capabilities, and expectations can lead to a series of microaggressions against the children. Some early childhood teachers admit to being unaware of the prejudices they hold toward other cultures, misunderstanding white privilege, and not recognizing the social inequalities that exist based on race and ethnicity (Ukpokodu, 2002). Not only do some teachers lack experience and exposure to cultures different from their own, but many report feeling unprepared to work with students from racially and ethnically diverse backgrounds (Jean-Sigur, Bell, and Kim, 2015). Additionally, Irvine (2003) found that many preservice teachers have negative beliefs and low expectations of success for students of color.

Adopting a color-blind ideology means pretending that teachers do not have racial biases and ignoring the racial disparities in education (Neville, Gallardo, and Sue, 2016). A color-blind ideology allows teachers to deny the racism that is endemic in our educational institutions and plays an integral part in racial inequities found in American schools (Beeman, 2015). Children have different needs based on their experiences and backgrounds; therefore, applying a color-blind approach is problematic because it does not allow children to receive the equitable support and resources they need to thrive in school.

What about Meritocracy?

Like color blindness, the concept of meritocracy can also be problematic, as it ignores systemic and institutional racism that privileges white people and disprivileges people of color. The notion of meritocracy is a core American value. America has prided itself on being the "land of opportunity." The narrative of working hard and "pulling oneself up by the bootstraps" is a widely held ideal among many Americans. Such individuals strongly believe that people get what they deserve in life based on their merit and hard work. *Meritocracy* refers to those who possess power based on their ability, skill, talent, and hard work (Hinchey, 2010). The idea of meritocracy is challenged by many critical race theorists.

Let's pause briefly to define and discuss critical race theory. Critical race theory (CRT) posits that racism and white privilege are deeply enmeshed in American society and that institutionalized racism is normal (Delgado and Stefancic, 2012). Gloria Ladson-Billings (1998) describes five aspects of CRT:

✦ Racism is deeply enmeshed in American culture.

✦ The incorporation of storytelling as a means for analyzing the myths of objectivity that surround American culture and laws in regard to race. The notions of meritocracy and color blindness are challenged.

✦ Liberalism and the civil rights movement largely benefited white Americans more than African Americans.

✦ A commitment to social justice is a priority.

✦ White people will support racial justice only if they benefit from it.
(This concept is called *interest convergence*.)

CRT provides a framework for critically analyzing structural racism. The theory challenges social structures and hierarchies that oppress African Americans and other people of color. Critical race theory is not "reverse racism." It's not anti-white or anti-American. Rather, it is a tool for understanding human inequality and creating equitable structures within society.

The notion of meritocracy suggests that an individual's status in life is attributed to their talents, hard work, merits, and abilities. While hard work accounts for some "success," the flaw with the notion of meritocracy is that it fails to account for oppressive and discriminatory practices rooted in institutional racism that often keep marginalized groups of color and other minorities oppressed. Critical race theory recognizes that the notion of meritocracy is often upheld by those in power who tell stories about their "hard work" (Ladson-Billings, 1998). Countering the notion of meritocracy is central to critical race theory as it gives voice to those who are often silenced by white supremacy culture (*Dixson and Rousseau, 2006*).

Understanding Implicit Bias

Along with color blindness and meritocracy, implicit racial biases also play a significant role in the cultural disconnect between home and school. Cheryl Staats, senior researcher at the Kirwan Institute for the Study of Race and Ethnicity, defines *implicit bias* as "the attitudes or stereotypes that affect our understanding, actions, and decisions in an unconscious manner" (Staats, 2015). Staats says that the implicit associations we hold influence our feelings and attitudes toward people based on characteristics such as race, age, and physical appearance.

Researcher Nilanjana Dasgupta (2013) contends that implicit biases develop early in life through socialization and are often influenced by our social environments. Our implicit biases are shaped by our experiences and result from a lack of exposure to other cultures and groups of people. Negative media imagery often reinforces stereotypes that influence our perceptions and beliefs about others (Dunham, Baron, and Banaji, 2008). Many of us have internalized these negative messages, which thus influence how we perceive and ultimately respond to and interact with others.

These unconscious biases influence how early childhood teachers perceive, respond, and interact with young children. Consider the following key characteristics of implicit bias:

✦ We all have implicit biases (Greenwald, McGhee, and Schwartz, 1998). Implicit biases are separate constructs from the explicit biases we hold and may be in direct contrast with our declared beliefs (Graham and Lowery, 2004).

✦ Implicit biases tend to favor our own group.

✦ Implicit biases have real-world effects on behavior (Dasgupta, 2004).

Let's look at an example of how our implicit biases operate.

Ebonyse's Experience

One afternoon I picked up my mother's prescription from CVS Pharmacy. We had been at the doctor's office all morning and early afternoon, and we were hungry when we left. In addition to getting her medication, I grabbed a few granola bars to snack on. A very pleasant middle-aged white woman greeted me at the counter and asked if I had found everything I needed. I smiled and answered yes. I said, "I have two cards that I am using to make this purchase." She told me that was okay.

She rang me up, and I asked how much I owed for the medication. She responded, "Just swipe your EBT card, sweetie. The system will separate the food from the medication." I was confused and angry—why did she assume I had an EBT card? I never said what type of card I had. I had mentioned only that I was using two cards to pay for the purchase. (In fact, I was using my mother's debit card to pay for her medication and my debit card to pay for the granola bars.) I responded, "I do not have an EBT card. I have two debit cards. Why did you assume I had an EBT card?" She responded apologetically, "I am so sorry. I just assumed you were using an EBT card since you said you had two cards." I asked again, "But why did you make that assumption?" She said, "It was the way I was raised." I asked, "How was that? To assume that all African American women receive public assistance?" She responded, "I was raised to think that Black people are poor."

Surprisingly, she was very honest in her response. She apologized again and said, "I want to do better. I want to learn because I now have mixed-race grandchildren." I told her that her comment was not only inaccurate but hurtful. Not all African American women receive public assistance. She apologized again. I offered her my business card and told her that I facilitate training on implicit racial biases and suggested that perhaps the store could use a series of workshops. We talked a little more about the ways we have been raised to think about other people and how our implicit biases can influence the interactions we have with people. I stated how important it is to have exposure to other groups of people to challenge the assumptions we hold.

This experience, although hurtful for me, is not uncommon. Many African Americans experience implicit racial biases on a daily basis. However, it was a teachable moment for the clerk to think about the implicit biases she holds and the ways she can challenge those biases.

Implicit Bias and School-Discipline Practices

It is important to understand the role implicit racial bias plays in the often unequal outcomes experienced by African American children and other children of color when compared to their white counterparts. Research demonstrates that racial disparities are common in school-discipline practices (Fabelo et al., 2011; Okonofua and Eberhardt, 2015). In recent years, there has been a growing emphasis on the role of implicit racial bias in how schools discipline children of color and teachers' perceptions of children of color, particularly in relation to African American boys (Gilliam et al., 2016; McIntosh et al., 2014; Gibson et al., 2014; Goff et al., 2014; Skiba et al., 2011).

Studies on school suspension disparities have found that African American preschool children are three times more likely to be suspended than white students (U.S. Department of Education, 2014; Gregory et al. 2010; Milner, 2013). Losen and Martinez (2013) found that in the 2009–2010 school year, out-of-school suspensions of Black children occurred at a rate of 24.3 percent compared to a rate of 7.1 percent among white children. These disparities in suspensions are uniquely related to teachers' perceptions and beliefs about students. For example, in one study, white female undergraduate students were surveyed regarding their perceptions of African American children. In the study, photographs were shown with descriptions of various crimes. The respondents were asked to assess the age and innocence of African American, Latine, and white youths between the ages of ten and seventeen. Results revealed that respondents overestimated the age of African American youths by an average of four and a half years and found them more culpable than both Latine and white youth (Goff et al., 2014).

A similar study of youth, caregivers, and professionals found that the majority of participants viewed implicit racial biases and cultural differences as the main contributing factors for the disproportionate rates of African American students being suspended. These findings are consistent with other literature suggesting African American children are often criminalized, dehumanized, viewed as less innocent or "childlike," and treated more harshly than their white peers (Goff et al., 2014). Gilliam et al. (2016) found that when early childhood teachers are told to expect challenging behaviors, they more closely observe African American boys than white boys. Gilliam and colleagues (2016) also suggest that implicit biases may differ depending on the teacher's race. Other research demonstrates racial bias in how teachers perceive African American children. Okonofua and Eberhardt (2015) found that when African American and white children are engaged in similar unwanted behaviors, teachers regularly identify the behaviors of African American children as less tolerable than the behaviors of their white peers based on stereotypes. These studies suggest that teachers' implicit racial biases influence their perceptions of African American children, especially when challenging behaviors are concerned (Gilliam et al., 2016; Okonofua and Eberhardt, 2015).

These negative perceptions held by education professionals often influence how they respond to, interact with, and discipline African American children and other children of color. In addition, teachers' implicit racial biases can adversely affect children's self-concept and self-worth as they internalize negative messages of unworthiness and develop a sense of shame. A report from the Office of Child Development at the University of Pittsburgh contends that too often children of color, particularly African American children, experience daily messages from individuals and institutions that they are not good enough, not as smart, or not as beautiful as white children (White and Wanless, 2019).

Cultural Disconnects in Education

The cultural disconnect in our system is fueled by a European-American worldview in education, including early childhood education. The content of teacher education programs is often based on white European and American theorists, such as Jean Piaget, Lev Vygotsky, Albert Bandura, and Erik Erikson, who are often cited in programs meant to prepare teachers to understand children's development. While these theories are valid, they do not reflect the worldview of racially and ethnically diverse children. They do not consider the impact racism has on the development of African American children and other children of color. African American children are more likely to live in poverty, attend underresourced schools, and have less access to high-quality health care and early childhood programs (Tileston 2010; Milner, 2013; York, 2016). Because children exist within the context of their families and communities, it is imperative to understand that societal and environmental influences such as a lack of access to healthy foods, police violence against people of color, inadequate health care, inferior schools, and poor housing can have a major impact on children's learning and development. Children and families of color are more likely to experience these social ills because of structural and institutional racism; therefore, understanding the impact racism has on children's development is critical.

The European-American orientation of early learning programs overlooks the perspectives of other cultural groups that are traditionally marginalized or isolated. See the table on page 29 for a comparison of early learning environments with a European-American orientation and an environment with a culturally responsive orientation.

Derman-Sparks, LeeKeenan, and Nimmo (2015) explain that even when the majority of the children and families served in an early childhood education program are from a diverse background, the European-American dominant culture is the orientation in which children are being educated. For example, developmental screenings such as the Ages and Stages Questionnaire (ASQ), state early learning standards, grades, and assessments such as the Classroom

Assessment Scoring System (CLASS) were developed by white individuals operating within a white European-American worldview. These tools, used to guide and measure children's development and learning, are rooted in a European-American orientation of individualism and competition. This is not to suggest these early learning standards, screenings, and assessments are not useful, but they are created from a worldview that does not consider African American children and other children of color.

Barnes (2006) states, "This cultural disconnect between early childhood teacher education programs, teachers, and the culturally and linguistically diverse children and families they serve produces negative interactions between teachers and students, thus reinforcing stereotypes and prejudices." Addressing the cultural disconnect requires a deep and thorough exploration into white supremacy culture, deconstructing whiteness within education, and examining the role racism has on children's learning and development.

Comparison of Early Learning Environments

European-American Orientation of Early Learning Programs	Culturally Responsive, Anti-Bias Early Learning Programs
Individualistic	Individualistic within the group (focused on the collective)
Rule driven	Freedom loving
Controlled	Expressive
Rigid (order focused)	Flexible
Conformist	Creative
Standardized	Variation accepting

(Sullivan, 2016)

REFLECTING ON THE CULTURAL DISCONNECT IN EARLY CHILDHOOD EDUCATION

✦ How have you seen this cultural disconnect show up in your school or program?

✦ In what ways can the cultural disconnect affect teacher-child relationships?

✦ How might you mitigate the cultural disconnect in your classroom, school, or program?

CHAPTER 3

Supporting a Socially Just Early Childhood Workforce

One of the findings from Ebonyse's dissertation study was that many teachers want and need more professional development and training in culturally responsive anti-bias (CRAB) education.

York (2016) describes CRAB "as the most current term for a comprehensive approach to multicultural education in early childhood settings." This approach:

✦ addresses culture, diversity, fairness, and social action;

✦ seeks to reduce prejudice; and

✦ encourages caregiving practices that complement families' styles of caring for their children.

One of the most common misconceptions about CRAB is that it is only beneficial for children of color. On the contrary, CRAB is beneficial for all children. Research tells us that children are not color-blind, and they develop racial preferences and biases as early as the age of three (Winkler, 2009). This is all the more reason CRAB should be incorporated into the daily experience of the classroom. Remember that culturally responsive anti-bias education:

✦ recognizes the importance of including children's cultures into all aspects of learning;

✦ creates learning environments where all students are welcomed, valued, and feel safe learning, regardless of their cultural and linguistic backgrounds;

✦ builds positive racial and ethnic identity development in young children; and focuses on teaching equity and social justice.

REFLECTING ON CRAB EDUCATION

Considering what you now know about the CRAB approach, take a moment to reflect on the following questions.

✦ In what ways are you already implementing CRAB practices into your classrooms or the educational program?

✦ What lesson plans or activities can you develop that will help reduce prejudice among young children?

✦ How do you incorporate different families' styles of caring into your care and education of young children?

Learning in a Community of Practice

Now that we have a better understanding of culturally responsive anti-bias education, let's turn our attention to peer-to-peer learning through a community of practice. Supporting teachers in becoming culturally responsive and equity-minded educators requires more than attending one or two professional development workshops on CRAB. Ongoing training and coaching is needed to change behaviors and instructional practices. Engaging in continuous, collaborative learning to inform practice allows early childhood educators the opportunity to stay current and abreast with trends, research, and best practices. Peer-to-peer learning through a community of practice is a common approach taken to help transform instructional practices. A community of practice is simply a group of people—in this case, educators—who work together to learn about a topic that they believe will help them improve their work.

Communities of practice (CoPs) are defined as "groups of people who share a concern or a passion for a topic and deepen their knowledge and expertise in this area by interaction on an ongoing basis (Wenger, McDermott, and Snyder, 2002). Communities of practice related to promoting equitable learning environments allow teachers to purposefully interact with each other to hone their skills in integrating CRAB practices into the learning environment. They are able to challenge their implicit racial biases and the practices that perpetuate inequitable outcomes for children. Because the journey of racial equity is not a fixed or set destination, a community of practice is an ideal approach for teachers to sharpen their skills in culturally responsive anti-bias education.

Consistent coaching, consultation, and modeling are necessary to help teachers change behaviors and instructional practices. Applying transformative learning theory can be a valuable strategy to help educators become culturally responsive professionals and incorporate CRAB practices within their classrooms. *Transformative learning theory* is a theory of adult learning developed by the late Jack Mezirow, a professor at Teachers College at Columbia University. The theory asserts that all individuals have a particular view of the world that is shaped by their experiences (familial, cultural, societal, and more). This worldview is based on assumptions that are deeply ingrained in the individual and become unconscious frames of reference (Christie et al., 2015).

Because these assumptions (or worldviews) are deeply embedded in the individual, Mezirow argues it will take an activating event or, as he refers to it, a *distorting dilemma* to help change the individual's worldview. Let's look at an example of transformative learning theory in practice.

> *Ms. Paige, a kindergarten teacher, attended the Educational Equity Institute's Race Equity Summer Learning Program. The session on Challenging Our Implicit Racial Bias was very enlightening and eye-opening for Ms. Paige. In the session, she learned that people of color cannot, by definition, be racist, but they can perpetuate and internalize racist ideas. She learned that because people of color do not have collective institutional power, such as economic, political, or social power, they cannot oppress another group. They can, however, demonstrate prejudice. Prejudice and racism are not the same. This was new information to her because she's been conditioned to think that all people can be racist.*

+ **Original assumption/current worldview:** *Ms. Paige believed that people of color could be racist.*

+ **Activating event (distorting dilemma):** *Ms. Paige learned that although people of color can perpetuate racist ideas, they cannot be racist because they do not have the collective institutional power to oppress another group. This new information challenged Ms. Paige's original worldview.*

+ **Changed worldview:** *Ms. Paige understands those with collective and institutional power can oppress other groups of people.*

For transformative learning to take place, an individual is exposed to a situation that challenges their current worldview. This challenge prompts the individual to question their current worldview and consider an alternative or new perspective. Transformative learning begins as individuals undergo a process of critical self-reflection. This process requires an exploration into understanding where their assumptions came from and how those assumptions influence or restrict their understanding. Critical dialogue with peers and colleagues about alternative or new perspectives, and opportunities to test and apply these new perspectives and knowledge, are integral components of transformative learning theory (Cranton, 2016). This is why transformative learning theory is an ideal method to use in a community of practice to help teachers incorporate CRAB practices.

Using transformative learning as an approach in a community of practice can help teachers become culturally responsive educators. Through reflection, application, and implementation, early childhood educators can incorporate an equity pedagogy into their teaching. Adopting an equity pedagogy requires educators to understand the ways in which institutional racism has created inequitable outcomes for children of color in education. When educators adopt an equity pedagogy, they are careful to create environments that do not perpetuate harm through policies and practices that view children of color through a deficit lens. They are mindful that all children, regardless of their cultural background and linguistic ability, can learn and be successful.

Participating in a community of practice allows teachers to engage in opportunities to critically reflect upon and analyze new content related to culturally responsive anti-bias education as it is being introduced. Teachers need the opportunity to engage with new content through journaling, dialogue, and a process of critical self-reflection, during which they examine their own cultures, identities, biases, assumptions, and beliefs.

In the next phase of application and implementation, teachers engage in opportunities for deeper understandings of race, racism, power, privilege, and oppression and the need to incorporate culturally responsive anti-bias education. Teachers need to fully understand the interlocking economic, political, and social that sustain racial inequalities for children of color in our educational system. They need to understand how power, privilege, and racism have historically shown up, and currently show up, in our institutions and perpetuate inequalities based on race, class, and gender. Teachers must have opportunities to act on new perspectives through coaching and continuous learning as they begin to incorporate culturally responsive anti-bias education into their teaching practice.

Teachers need support in being intentional about disrupting practices and policies that maintain systems of oppression and applying new skills and knowledge that promote racial equity. As teachers are going through the perspective transformation process, the community of practice is an ideal space to process and reflect as new information is being constructed, resources are being shared, and connections are being made.

Transformative learning is an intentional process that takes time. Because this process requires teachers to reflect on their assumptions and biases about race and culture and to challenge or change their worldviews to embrace more culturally responsive practices, the process of transformation can often be uncomfortable and emotionally charged. It will be important for teachers to be kind to themselves, demonstrate patience, and commit to nonclosure. Committing to *nonclosure* requires teachers to be mindful that the work of creating equitable early learning programs does not happen overnight but rather over time. It takes a considerable amount of patience, time, and learning to celebrate the small wins.

Let's return to the case of Ms. Paige and with a vignette that demonstrates how transformative learning theory works in a community of practice

Ms. Paige has completed the Race Equity Summer Learning Program, and she has new knowledge that has challenged her current worldview. She participates in a four-week community of practice with the cohort of learners from the program. The group is asked to keep a journal of their thoughts and reflections for the four weeks as a way of continuing to process the new information. In the first week, the group discusses what resonated with them from the training workshops, what information was new, what was challenging, and what questions they still have. Through this process of reflection alongside her peers, Ms. Paige is able to work through the new information learned, take the perspectives of her colleagues into consideration, and make meaningful connections.

In the second week, the group is asked to reflect on their own cultural identity, assumptions, and biases, and how they show up as cultural beings. CoP members respond to reflection questions such as the following:

+ *What biases and assumptions do you hold about people of a different race/ethnicity than your own?*

+ *Why do you believe you hold these biases?*

+ *Where do you think these biases came from?*

+ *How have these biases influenced your interactions with culturally and linguistically diverse children and families?*

+ *In what ways can you challenge the biases you hold?*

CoP members are also asked to reflect on the ways racism, bias, and discrimination show up in the educational system and to think about ways they have unintentionally perpetuated racial bias or discrimination.

Through this process of critical reflection, Ms. Paige is developing a deeper understanding of the ways racism is deeply embedded in the American educational system. Her current worldview is being challenged as she thinks about the disproportionate rates at which preschool children of color, and African American children in particular, are suspended and expelled; the overrepresentation of children of color in special education; and the disproportionate rates at which children with special needs are suspended. Ms. Paige has never thought about the role of race in education before, but attending the race equity institute and being in community with her colleagues has given her a new perspective. This process of deep reflection allows Ms. Paige not only to challenge her own assumptions but also to listen to her colleagues and think about new approaches to solving educational inequities.

In the third week, CoP members are asked to create a culturally responsive anti-bias activity promoting children's positive racial and ethnic identity. This step in the transformative learning process is the implementation step, which gives Ms. Paige the opportunity to take the knowledge learned and put it into practice. The CoP members discuss the criteria for a culturally responsive anti-bias activity, such as including the child's cultural heritage in the activity. The members are able to learn from each other through sharing ideas and exchanging resources, thus building their capacity to be culturally responsive educators.

During week four, the members exchange their activities to receive feedback from their colleagues. This peer-to-peer strategy allows each member to craft constructive feedback to their peers.

This collective learning creates a sense of community and fosters a bond among colleagues. It also deepens and enriches the learning experiences of the members through shared learning and collaboration. The community of practice allows early childhood professionals to engage in dialogue about racial inequities in early childhood, reflect on personal biases and assumptions, share culturally responsive practices and supports, and advocate to advance racial equity in early childhood programs. The community of practice also provides opportunities to engage in conversations with peers about lessons learned, challenges, and strategies that work well. Supporting a socially just early childhood workforce will take a transformative learning approach that includes:

✦ a deep understanding of the root causes of educational inequities;

✦ a true commitment to lasting change in education;

✦ time, grace, and patience; and

✦ continued learning, development, and growth to change practices, policies, and behaviors.

REFLECTING ON DEVELOPING A COMMUNITY OF PRACTICE

✦ Have you ever participated in a community of practice? If so, what was your experience like? If not, would you consider participating?

✦ What other benefits can you think may result from participating in a community of practice?

✦ What challenges do you foresee, and how can you work through them?

Building Authentic Family Partnerships with Racially and Ethnically Diverse Families

Research suggests that family engagement in early childhood programs is very important to the educational success of young children, especially for children from culturally and linguistically diverse and lower socioeconomic backgrounds (Fantuzzo et al. 2004; Bryk and Schneider, 2003). However, despite good intentions, many early childhood professionals continue to struggle in their efforts to successfully engage racially, ethnically, and socioeconomically diverse families. Many programs attempt to engage these families with traditional methods of parental involvement such as parent-teacher conferences or back-to-school nights. Gillanders, McKinney, and Ritchie (2012) argue that such traditional methods of parental involvement are often school centered and fail to take into consideration the beliefs, goals, interests, and life circumstances of racially and ethnically diverse families. Traditional methods of parental involvement are often rooted in a middle-class white European-American worldview and fail to account for the life experiences, cultures, and circumstances of families of color (York, 2016).

Engagement with racially and ethnically diverse families has presented several challenges in many school settings. Research shows that teachers are more likely to contact Black and Latine families when children have behavioral issues than they are to report something positive about the child (Cherng, 2016). Additionally, racially and ethnically diverse families' practices of engagement are often not respected and sometimes even pathologized because they do not align with how many schools believe families should be engaged (Kubota and Lin, 2009). Many families feel they are ignored or dismissed because they already have a "problem" label when they mention concerns (Ishimaru, 2019). Moreover, these families may experience cultural mistrust because of their own negative school experiences, thus impacting their ability to authentically engage with teachers and the school as a whole.

Morrison (2008) encourages early childhood programs to consider how the cultural disconnect between home and school may inhibit a family's collaboration. In the next section, we'll explore barriers to engaging racially and ethnically diverse families.

Barriers to Engaging Racially and Ethnically Diverse Families

Transportation, time, and child care are just a few of the barriers to engaging families. However, racially and ethnically diverse families also experience other barriers, such as cultural disconnect, a culturally dominant perspective, implicit racial bias, a cultural-deficit model, and cultural mistrust.

Cultural Disconnect

As discussed in chapter 1, cultural disconnect is an issue that must be addressed to create equitable learning environments for children. Many early childhood teachers, particularly in the K–3 grades, are white, non-Hispanic, monolingual, and middle class (Banks and Banks, 2001; Gitanjali, Early, and Clifford, 2002). In addition, these teachers often lack experience and exposure to children from racially and ethnically diverse backgrounds (Hollins and Guzman, 2005) and may not be comfortable discussing race (Gay and Howard, 2001). Because the worldviews and cultural experiences of these teachers are vastly different from the racially and ethnically diverse students in their care, it is imperative that teachers and directors are intentional about establishing authentic and meaningful relationships with families of color.

Culturally Dominant Perspective

In addition to cultural disconnect, a culturally dominant perspective is another barrier. Because the American educational system is rooted in whiteness, a white middle-class worldview serves as the yardstick by which children and families of color are measured. The dominant cultural perspective or worldview sets the standard for how children should behave and how families should engage with schools. This worldview of whiteness is often not reflective or inclusive of the beliefs, behaviors, and practices of families of color.

Implicit Bias

Additionally, implicit racial bias plays a significant role as a barrier to authentically engaging racially and ethnically diverse families. Because racism is deeply enmeshed in our society, we have internalized both positive and negative racialized messages about other racial and ethnic groups. These internalized messages influence our perceptions and interactions with others. *Implicit biases* are the unconscious beliefs, attitudes, and perceptions that we hold that have the potential to affect our interactions, decisions, and responses to others. Our implicit biases are pervasive and robust, often develop early in life through socialization, and do not necessarily align with our declared beliefs. Additionally, the media often reinforce the negative stereotypes we have internalized about certain groups of people.

In education, implicit racial biases impact disciplinary practices, as Black preschool children are 3.6 times more likely than their white peers to be suspended (U.S. Department of Education, 2016). Implicit bias is also a contributing factor to the overrepresentation of culturally and linguistically diverse children in special education (Counts, Katsiyannis, and Whitford, 2018). Other literature on implicit racial bias demonstrates teachers' negative perception of Black children. As previously stated, research suggests that Black children are criminalized, dehumanized, viewed as less innocent, and treated more harshly than their white peers (Goff et al., 2014). Okonofua and Eberhardt (2015) found that when Black and white children are engaged in similar unwanted behaviors, teachers regularly respond to the behaviors of Black children as less tolerable than those of their white peers based on stereotypes. Educators must examine their own worldview when they are interacting with students and families of different cultural, linguistic, and socioeconomic backgrounds. We must be determined not only to unearth our own biases, but also to challenge them.

Cultural-Deficit Model

Similarly, we have to challenge the cultural-deficit model. The cultural-deficit model is a belief held by some educators that some families are lacking in the resources, skills, or talents necessary to support their children in their education (Grant and Ray, 2013). This model also blames families and students of color for the students' poor academic performance. The problem with this model is that it fails to account for the institutional barriers that families of color have to contend with to support their children's learning and development.

Cultural Mistrust

Another barrier is cultural mistrust. The term *cultural mistrust,* first described in Grier and Cobbs's book *Black Rage* (1968), is an adaptive attitudinal response to historical and personal oppression in which people of color are skeptical of trusting white people in institutional, personal, and social contexts, especially white people in positions of authority (Terrell and Terrell, 1981). Cultural mistrust is adaptive because it is a coping mechanism people of color use for survival and protection against racism and discrimination.

REFLECTING ON CuLTuRAL MISTRuST

How can cultural mistrust impact authentic engagement efforts with racially and ethnically diverse families?

Past experiences—whether personal, familial, or as members of a racial or ethnic group—can affect how families engage in the school environment and how educators engage with families. Cultural mistrust can negatively affect family engagement when:

✦ families initially meet with educational professionals,

✦ educational professionals work to build rapport with families, and

✦ educational professionals try to maintain relationships and establish authentic partnerships.

Weaker relationships between families and teachers due to cultural mistrust can then result in a decline in services and programs offered.

New Strategies for Family Engagement

When working with racially, ethnically, and socioeconomically diverse families, it is imperative that early childhood programs commit to developing a greater understanding of families' cultures, needs, and beliefs so that families feel included and respected.

Existing literature suggests that a family's culture and socioeconomic status can influence their level of engagement in early childhood programs. For example, Wildenger and McIntyre (2011) investigated parental involvement during kindergarten transitions. Their findings revealed that lower-income families participated in fewer transition-to-kindergarten activities. Jarret and Coba-Rodriguez (2015) interviewed nineteen low-income African American mothers of children enrolled in Head Start. The authors concluded that work schedules were a significant factor that prohibited parents' involvement because their work schedules did not align with the times of school events.

Gillanders, McKinney, and Ritchie (2012) conducted focus groups with African American and Latina mothers to learn what types of family engagement activities best fit their needs, beliefs about education, and goals for their children. The researchers concluded that families are more inclined to be engaged when activities and events reflect their cultural backgrounds. Similarly, Calzada and colleagues (2015) examined parental involvement among Afro-Caribbean and Latine immigrant families and found that families demonstrated increased involvement when parents felt that the activities were connected to their culture.

Racially and ethnically diverse families want to be engaged in their children's education. However, for families to be truly engaged, schools must learn to create authentic relationships with these families based on respect and trust. Engaging racially and ethnically diverse families using culturally responsive practices will help to build authentic and meaningful school and family partnerships. According to Grant and Ray (2013), culturally responsive family engagement involves practices that respect and acknowledge the cultural uniqueness, life experiences, and viewpoints of families and draws on those experiences to establish respectful partnerships. When educators understand aspects of the family's culture, they will not only better understand children's learning and development but also build stronger partnerships.

Diversity-Informed Tenets

Another practice-based approach to engaging racially and ethnically diverse families is the Diversity-Informed Tenets. The tenets, developed by the Irving Harris Foundation, are guiding principles that raise awareness about inequities and injustices embedded in our society. The tenets allow individuals working with or supporting young children and their families to place equity and inclusion at the center of their work by being intentional in addressing those inequities that are deeply embedded within our systems.

TEN DIVERSITY-INFORMED TENETS

1. Self-awareness leads to better services for families.

2. Champion children's rights globally.

3. Work to acknowledge privilege and combat discrimination.

4. Recognize and respect nondominant bodies of knowledge.

5. Honor diverse family structures.

6. Understand that language can hurt or heal.

7. Support families in their preferred language.

8. Allocate resources to system change.

9. Make space and open pathways.

10. Advance policy that supports all families.

(Irving B. Harris Foundation, n.d.)

There are ten Diversity-Informed Tenets; however, for the purposes of this chapter, we will discuss only the five tenets that are specifically relevant to supporting culturally responsive relationships.

Self-awareness leads to better services for families: Racial-equity work requires a significant amount of self-reflection and evaluation. As educators, we must reflect on our cultures, assumptions, and beliefs, particularly when it comes to how they affect our decisions, interactions, and relationships. We must acknowledge how discriminatory practices and policies perpetuate inequitable outcomes for children and families.

Work to acknowledge privilege and combat discrimination: We all hold some form of privilege, whether it is based on our race, gender, class, nationality, language, religion, or ability. To create equitable environments as educators, we must acknowledge privilege where we hold it and use our privilege to create inclusive spaces and challenge inequitable practices and policies that produce disparities for children and families.

Recognize and respect nondominant bodies of knowledge: We must acknowledge and respect family strengths and view families as assets and sources of strengths. We must approach our interactions with families from a strengths-based perspective as opposed to a deficit perspective. We must also respect families' funds of knowledge. All families have specific ways of raising children, problem solving, communicating, and more that are based on their cultural practices. Their ways of being and functioning may look different from our own. It doesn't mean one way is right or better—it's simply different. Despite the adversities families may experience, we must respect each family's funds of knowledge as a fundamental component of who they are.

Honor diverse family structures: Today's early learning programs and classrooms are becoming increasingly diverse in family structure, culture, language, race, ethnicity, socioeconomic status, religion, and sexual orientation. Because classrooms are increasingly diverse, educators are being called to develop the knowledge and skills to equitably and effectively partner with *all* families.

Support families in their preferred language: Supporting families in their preferred language shows families that they are valued and that their culture and language are respected.

Applying these five diversity-informed tenets creates a pathway for educators to develop culturally responsive relationships that will strengthen school and family partnerships.

REFLECTING ON THE DIVERSITY-INFORMED TENETS

✦ Which of the ten diversity-informed tenets resonates with you the most, and why?

✦ Which tenet do you think is most useful in supporting culturally responsive engagement practices?

Practical Strategies to Promote Inclusivity

As early childhood classrooms become more culturally diverse, it is essential to emphasize being inclusive of all families. The following strategies are offered to help early childhood programs engage all families, particularly those from cultural, linguistically, and socioeconomic backgrounds that differ from the dominant group.

✦ Conduct a cultural audit of your classroom.

✦ Develop authentic, trusting relationships with families by conducting regular home visits.

✦ Host a cultural night at the school, and invite parents to share their family's cultural heritage and background.

✦ Attend a neighborhood or community event to gain a better and deeper understanding of the community.

✦ Host school events in the community rather than in the school.

Conduct a Classroom Cultural Audit

Grant and Ray (2013) suggest conducting a classroom cultural audit that involves reviewing classroom displays such as bulletin boards, children's books, the curriculum, and so on to ensure that there is diversity throughout the classroom environment. Pay attention to differences such as age, gender, ability, race, ethnicity, religion, and social class. The goal is to make all children and families feel both included and welcomed.

Conduct Regular Home Visits

Conducting home visits with families provides teachers the opportunity to see families in their natural environment and helps parents stay in their comfort zone. These home visits are not meant to judge or critique a family for how they are living. These visits are meant to strengthen the relationships between teachers and parents or caregivers, which will allow the teacher and parent or caregiver to work together to create the best learning environment in which the child can thrive and be successful. Visiting families at home conveys the message that teachers are invested in the child's education and in collaborating with parents or caregivers.

Host a Cultural Night and Invite Family Participation

Families can share cultural artifacts, food, or other items representative of their cultures (such as a special cooking pot like a Moroccan tagine or tortilla press or an article of clothing like a scarf or headwrap or a jingle dress).

Attend a Neighborhood or Community Event

Children and families exist in the context of the communities in which they live. Having a better understanding of the family's neighborhood and community can help teachers make meaningful connections with families. For example, teachers can better understand the intimate connections families have with their communities and how communities are equipped to support families.

Host School Events in the Community

Hosting school events in the community may be a particularly useful strategy for those families with transportation barriers. For example, replace parent-teacher conferences with parent-teacher café conversations. Parents often feel intimidated by parent-teacher conferences. Therefore, reframing the purpose of the meeting to be more conversational and less formal may increase family engagement.

Because families are dynamic, the types and levels of engagement will vary for each family. Early childhood programs should expect family engagement to look different for each family based on their cultural needs, preferences, beliefs, and life circumstances. Tileston (2010) encourages educators to recognize and respect the cultural differences in students and their families. The goal of family engagement is to partner with families. It is important that early childhood programs understand that many low-income families may already feel excluded and marginalized because of their cultural and linguistic backgrounds. Early childhood programs can serve as a welcoming place where parents, caregivers, and families feel connected, supported, valued, and respected when the appropriate strategies are used.

Developing authentic, trusting relationships with families is a must to foster strong school and family partnerships. Teachers and early childhood leaders must go beyond traditional methods of family involvement, become culturally responsive, and develop engagement strategies that are suitable to families' cultural and life circumstances. Family engagement in early childhood programs is more than parents attending parent-teacher conferences or volunteering in the classroom. It is about creating opportunities where families are seen as equal partners and are integral in actively supporting the learning and development of their young children.

REFLECTING ON PROMOTING INCLUSIVITY

✦ Does your classroom welcome all families regardless of their cultural, linguistic, or socioeconomic background? If so, in what ways?

✦ What specific strategies have you implemented to intentionally engage families in your program? In what ways do families share their cultures with the classroom and program?

CHAPTER 5

Understanding Racially and Ethnically Diverse Learners

Ebonyse's Experience

During family gatherings, it was common for my grandmother to bake several desserts and for my mother, older aunts, and cousins to pull out the card table and play Bid Whist, a game played with playing cards. Growing up in Chicago, during the summer it was customary to find my best girlfriends and me jumping Double Dutch. For holidays, it was a tradition that my mother pressed and curled my hair using a hot comb. These cultural experiences shaped me as a child and influenced who I am as a Black woman.

Culture, inextricably ingrained in who we are, is a significant part of our identity and influences our beliefs, values, and social interactions. *Culture* is defined as the norms, values, practices, patterns of communication, laws, language, customs, and meanings shared by a group of people located in a given time and place (Sensoy and DiAngelo, 2017). Often when we think about culture, we think about our racial and ethnic backgrounds, but culture is more than that. Our culture also consists of our geographic location, our community or neighborhood, even our workplace culture. Considering culture beyond race and ethnicity can help to create more equitable learning environments for children.

Examining Cultural Identities in the Classroom

As early learning programs and classrooms become more racially, linguistically, and ethnically diverse, it is incumbent upon early childhood teachers and directors to examine their cultural identities and how their cultural backgrounds may differ from those of the students in their care. Because culture serves as a framework for how we view the world, including our thoughts about education, teachers must reflect on how their culture influences their ability to teach and lead. Davis (2007) points out that when teachers understand their own cultural lens, they can better honor and respect the cultures of students in their classrooms. For example, the holidays celebrated, the customs and norms about parenting and caring for the elderly, concepts of time and notions of beauty, the specific foods eaten, and the different languages are all examples of aspects of a person's cultural identities.

REFLECTING ON CULTURAL AWARENESS

Reflect on your culture—racial, ethnic, linguistic, geographical, religious/spiritual, and so on. Now reflect on the cultures of the students in your care. On a sheet of paper, make three columns:

1. List as many of your cultural identities as you can think of in the first column.

2. In the second column, write down the cultural identities of your students (as many as you may know).

3. List the cultural identities you have in common in the third column.

Save this paper, and as you get to know more about your students and their families, go back and add what you have learned to the various columns.

Social Location

An important part of reflecting on your cultural identity is thinking about your social location. *Social location* is a term used primarily in the social sciences, but it is useful in developing a greater understanding of culture. Social location is the social position an individual holds within their society. Certain characteristics, such as social class, may be deemed more important in one society than in another. An individual's social location includes their race, ethnicity, social class, age, ability, religion, sexual orientation, and geographical location. In educating racially and ethnically diverse students, it is important for teachers and directors to acknowledge their own social location and reflect on how their social location may affect their approach to teaching and working with diverse learners. A teacher can reflect on how their race, family values, religion and/or faith, and even their geographic location influences their perspectives and ideas about teaching and learning. For instance, a teacher who has a family value of thinking of the consequences before acting may incorporate this family value into their instructional practices and pedagogy.

REFLECTING ON SOCIAL LOCATION: TEACHERS

Reflect on your social location: your race, ethnicity, social class, religious background, geographic location, and so on. How does your social location influence your instructional practices and the relationships you build with students in your care? In other words, do your racial background, religious beliefs, and other social identities influence the way you teach and interact with children?

REFLECTING ON SOCIAL LOCATION: DIRECTORS

How does your social location influence your interactions with teachers and the way you approach and interact with families? In other words, do your beliefs and social class influence the way you interact with families?

The Cultural Iceberg Model

The Cultural Iceberg model has been used frequently in the social sciences and education to help deepen our understanding of culture and help us become more culturally responsive. In 1976, Edward T. Hall used the iceberg as a metaphor to create the Cultural Iceberg model. Why an iceberg? Most of an iceberg's mass is underwater, where it is difficult to see. Hall identified three levels of culture:

✦ Level 1 is surface culture. It includes cultural aspects such as food, language, music, arts, dance, and so on.

✦ Level 2 is deep culture. It is behavior based and includes cultural aspects such as body language, eye contact, personal space, concepts of time, facial expressions, and so on (Sullivan, 2016).

✦ Level 3 is unconscious culture. It is values based and includes cultural aspects such as concepts of leadership, parenting, decision-making, marriage, and so on (Sullivan, 2016).

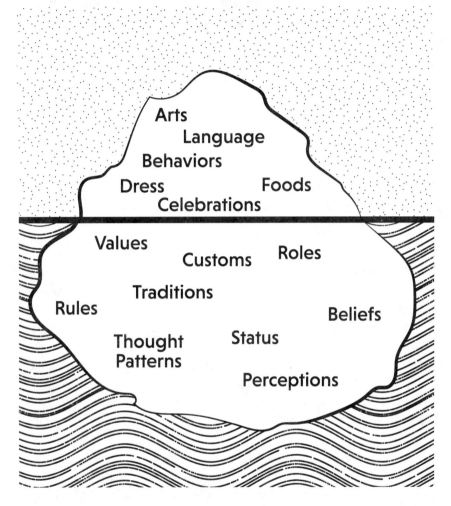

When we think about culture, we typically think of elements from level 1, the surface level—the tip of the iceberg. We typically think about food, language, artifacts, music, holidays, and so on. However, not enough attention is paid to either deep or unconscious culture, the items underneath the surface. These behaviors and values-based cultural items deeply shape our identity, our worldview, and how we show up as cultural beings. It is imperative for teachers and directors to have a working knowledge of the ways culture influences the learning and development of children of color at each level. For example, it has been consistently well documented that many Black students are more successful in learning environments where they can move about freely and be expressive, demonstrative, and spontaneous (Boykins, 1983; Hale, 1986; Hale, 2016; Sullivan, 2016; Howard, 2018). However, these behaviors may be seen as disruptive and inappropriate because they do not align with traditional expectations of how children should engage and behave in the classroom setting.

REFLECTING ON THE CULTURAL ICEBERG MODEL

Take a look at the image of the Cultural Iceberg. How often do you think about your students from the perspective of the cultural aspects in levels 2 and 3? In what ways can you be more intentional in thinking about your students from these sections?

The Impact of Culture on Intellectual and Social Development

Because European-American culture greatly influences the American educational system, including early childhood, it is likely that children of color feel isolated, excluded, or marginalized from the learning environment. European-American culture dictates educational policies, the curricula and assessments used, instructional practices, and the way preservice teachers are prepared. This cultural frame of reference often fails to support the unique learning styles of students of color. Culture is part and parcel of children's intellectual and social development. It greatly influences how children learn, problem solve, communicate, and interact; all of which are critically important both in and outside the classroom. Educators who understand children in the context of their cultures are able to create equitable learning environments for all children.

More than thirty years of research has focused on the cultural learning styles and preferences of students of color (Cox and Ramirez, 1981; Hale, 1986; Hilliard, 1989; Shade, 1989; Pewewardy, 2002; Vasquez, 1991). Additionally, educational researchers and scholars such as Gloria Ladson-Billings, Louise Derman-Sparks, Geneva Gay, Carol Brunson Day, and Stacey York have lent their voices to the discourse on multicultural and anti-bias education and culturally relevant teaching practices. Understanding the impact of culture on the learning styles of students of color is paramount in creating equitable learning environments where students can thrive.

York (2016) has identified several characteristics of European-American culture, including analytical thinking style, individualism, materialism, and self-responsibility/self-sufficiency. These characteristics are embedded within the American educational system.

Characteristics of European-American Culture	
Analytical thinking style	✦ People use logical, sequential thinking. ✦ People value rational and objective thinking that can be proven; subjective or intuitive knowledge is not highly valued.
Individualism	✦ People are unique individuals, distinct from their family or culture. ✦ People tend to value personal freedom, choice, and autonomy.
Materialism	✦ People place a high value on things such as clothing, cars, or houses. ✦ Owning goods contributes to an individual sense of self and status in the community and in life.
Self-responsibility/Self-sufficiency	✦ People are responsible for their own behavior and managing their own lives. ✦ Individuals should provide for their own basic needs and not rely on others.

(York, 2016)

Many of these characteristics are in contradiction to the cultural values of many peoples of color. For example, the self-responsibility and self-sufficiency characteristic is contradictory to the African American cultural value of *communalism*, which involves the priority of duty or commitment to one's social group over individual privileges (Boykin, 1994). In African American families, extended family networks and fictive kinship (a term used by sociologists for ties that are based on neither blood nor marriage relationships) are important to the family structure and family dynamics. It is common for African Americans to claim close family friends as familial relatives when there is no blood relation. For example, Ebonyse refers to her mother's best friend as her aunt. It is also commonplace for African Americans to refer to close family friends as "play cousins." The word *play* indicates the acknowledgment that there are no blood ties. However, despite the absence of any blood ties or marital connections, these close friends are family nonetheless. Extended family members play a significant role in helping African American families raise children and in caring for the overall well-being of the family. For example, when Ebonyse's parents worked the second shift, her grandmother cared for her at night. Before her son attended preschool, her mother cared for him during the day. "Multi-generation families and intergenerational kinships have played a significant role in preserving and strengthening African American families" (Waites, 2009).

Similarly, in Latine, Asian, Indigenous, and Hawaiian/Pacific Islander families, family interdependence and close family ties are also valued (Allen, Perrote, and Feinman, 2022; Osai and Fitisemanu, 2022; Hwang, 2022; Schvaneveldt, 2022). In Indigenous families, "family loyalty is strong" (Allen, Perrote, and Feinman, 2022). Extended family members such as grandparents, aunts and uncles, and great-aunts and -uncles play a significant role in raising children. They teach and pass on cultural traditions, strengths, and values to the younger generation. Elders in the Indigenous community are held in high regard. In Asian families, a strong sense of community and loyalty toward one's parents is valued. In many Asian families, "filial piety is an important virtue" (Hwang, 2022). *Filial piety* is an attitude of respect for parents, elders, and ancestors. Children demonstrate this virtue of respect by obeying their parents and caring for them as they age. Such close family ties are integral to Asian culture. In Latine families, family interdependence is a cultural norm. *Familismo* is rooted in collectivist orientations in which group goals are preferred over individual goals (Schvaneveldt, 2022). Family loyalty, closeness, and supporting and caring for family are deeply embedded within the Latine culture.

The European-American characteristics of individualism and self-responsibility/self-sufficiency are emphasized in many early learning programs. For example, personal freedom and autonomy are valued, and children are expected to take responsibility for themselves. This concept is in contrast to the collectivist/communal orientation of African Americans and other groups of color.

Another way to view these cultural characteristics is the differences between high context and low context cultures. These terms were developed by an anthropologist to categorize the ways in which different cultural groups interact, relate and learn. Below is a table to highlight some of the key differences between the two.

Comparison of High- and Low-Context Cultures

High Context (African American, Latine, Asian, Indigenous, and Hawaiian/Pacific Islander)	Low Context (European American)
Interaction ✦ Prefer nonverbal communication. Uses lots of facial expressions and gestures to convey meaning. ✦ The context of a discussion (people and situation involved) are more important. than the actual words.	**Interaction** ✦ Prefer verbal communication. Messages are explicit and direct. ✦ The actual words are more valuable than the context of a discussion.
Relationships ✦ Extremely important and frames an individual's identity. ✦ Strengthened overtime and founded on trust and collaboration. ✦ Clear boundaries of who does and does not belong within the group.	**Relationships** ✦ Identity is individually defined by personal achievement. ✦ Ever changing and may begin and end quickly. ✦ Boundaries are unclear and group membership is more open.
Learning ✦ Knowledge is gained through observation and hands-on experience. ✦ Group learning is preferred.	**Learning** ✦ Knowledge is gained through explicitly verbal instruction ✦ Individual learning is preferred

(Pfeiffer, 1993)

Preferred Learning Styles

Let's turn our attention to some of the research about the preferred learning styles of students of color. The following paragraphs will focus on Native American, African American, and Latine students, as these children often experience racial disparities within the educational system. As we consider preferred learning styles, it's important to avoid generalizing students. Generalizations about a group of people can lead to stereotypes that perpetuate inaccurate depictions and harmful messages. While it is important to have a working knowledge of the relationship between culture and the preferred learning styles of students of color, it is equally important to remember that students are both individuals and members of their respective racial and ethnic groups. There is no monolithic way to be African American,

Native American, or Latine. Racially and ethnically diverse learners possess unique learning styles based on both their individuality as people as well as membership in their racial or ethnic group.

Native American Students

Research suggests that Native American students tend to be reflective, visual, and cooperative learners (Swisher, 1991; Pewewardy, 2008; Morgan, 2009). These preferred learning styles are reflective of the cultural values and norms of indigenous people. Swisher (1991) argues that because many Native Americans value humility and harmony, these values influence the ways children from these cultures engage in the learning environment. For example, considering the importance placed on harmony, Native American students may not successfully perform tasks that other students cannot perform well to avoid being perceived as superior (Morgan, 2009). Learning through observation is common practice in Native American culture and should be considered when designing learning activities for Native students.

Psychologist Albert Bandura's social learning theory describes the ways in which children learn through observation and modeling. Bandura asserts that children are influenced by people in their lives, including parents, peers, and teachers; the neighborhoods they live in; and media, including television (Berk and Myers, 2016). As children observe the behaviors of those who influence them, they make mental notes about behaviors, store those mental notes in their memory, and may imitate the behaviors at a later time.

Native American students may often learn a new task or skill by observing someone in their family or culture. This learning through observation is in contrast with traditional teaching practices in American schools that encourage students to discover and problem solve on their own. Teachers should be mindful to create learning opportunities in which Native American students can learn through observation, such as matching and concentration activities. The teacher can demonstrate for children how to play the matching activity on a computer and then allow the children a turn to match the cards on the computer. As the teacher is modeling how to play the matching activity, the child is attuned to the teacher and thus learns how to imitate the teacher's actions. Knowing this cultural tendency can make a significant difference in the way Native American students engage in the learning environment and can strengthen teacher-student relations.

African American Students

There is a lot of research on the learning styles of African American students (Hale, 1986; Ladson-Billings, 1998; Hilliard, 1989; Irvine, 2003). The consistent theme throughout the research is the importance of understanding the culture of these students, which requires teachers and directors to look beyond the students' immediate community and neighborhood, to look deeper than slavery, and to begin in West Africa. Sullivan (2016) reminds us, "Black children come from a culture that is deeply rooted in West African tradition, values, and languages." African Americans value communal and extended family networks, creative expression, spirituality, and collaboration (Baugh and Coughlin, 2012; Sullivan, 2016). These values can be traced back to traditions and practices in West Africa. For example, dancing, playing drums, and weaving baskets are all examples of creative expression within West African culture.

To create equitable learning environments where Black children thrive, educators must deeply consider how these values can be intentionally integrated into the daily life of the classroom. Research suggests that many African American students prefer learning opportunities that are experiential, kinesthetic, and collaborative and allow them to express themselves creatively (Hilliard, 1976; Willis, 1989; Watkins, 2002; and Hale, 2016).

Hale (1986) contends that African American students' learning in the classroom and instruction environments relies upon cognitive, emotional, and physical engagement. Some African American students may need to feel a personal connection to the activity in order to be successful; others may need to manipulate or touch an object because tactile learning is preferred. As a teacher, it is important to know and understand the various ways African American children engage in the classroom and to tailor instruction so that it sets them up for success.

African American students tend to prefer learning by moving, doing, and touching. Similarly, they prefer opportunities to work in small groups and value opportunities where they can express themselves through dancing, singing, rapping, drawing, playing, art, and writing (Sullivan, 2016). Therefore, it is imperative to design lesson plans that incorporate learning opportunities for Black children to be tactile, creative, and collaborative. For example, scavenger hunts are an excellent way for African American students to engage in tactile learning where they can move around freely and learn by doing. Another example is helping African American children make playdough, which is a good way for students to learn through physical activity and through a sense of touch.

Latine Students

Like understanding the learning styles of Native American and African American children, understanding the learning styles and preferences of Latine students can be best understood in the context of their culture. Latine students represent both native-born and immigrant students and are from various locations, including Mexico, Puerto Rico, the Dominican Republic, Cuba, and countries in both Central and South America. Given the diversity within the Latine population, it is critical to understand the uniqueness of the cultures and avoid generalizations. It is also extremely important to know where Latine families are from originally or with which country they identify (Schvaneneldt and Behnke, 2012). When thinking about educating and working with Latine students, consider factors such as assimilation, acculturation, language, immigration status, and so on. It is also helpful to know how students identify—do they identify as Latino/a, Hispanic, Afro-Latino/a, or some other designation?

Before further exploring the learning styles and preferences of Latine students, let's review the terms *assimilated* and *acculturated*. Reviewing these terms helps educators have a better understanding of the factors that influence the lived experiences of many Latino/a students. There are some Latine students who have assimilated into the U.S. mainstream culture, and there are other students who are acculturated. People who are assimilated have adopted many of the dominant cultural values and retain little to no cultural traditions unique to their original culture (Schvaneneldt and Behnke, 2012). People who are acculturated, however, have developed more of a balance between their traditional culture and the dominant culture (Schvaneveldt and Behnke, 2012). Knowing the difference between these terms can help educators in establishing connections and relationships with children and families. Research on the population shows that family is often highly valued. There is a strong sense of responsibility for family members. Because the family is central to the Latine population, characteristics such as cooperation, loyalty, and commitment are important. Religion is also an important value within Latine populations (Schvaneveldt and Behnke, 2012).

Research shows that Latine students have a variety of learning preferences and styles, including kinesthetic and peer-oriented learning (Ewing and Yong, 1992; Sims, 1998; Griggs and Dunn, 1996). For these students, learning environments that offer a high degree of structure are often preferred (Ewing and Yong, 1992). Dunn, Griggs, and Price (1993) found that Mexican-American females were more peer oriented; Mexican-American males were found to be more authority oriented. Latine students were found to be field-dependent learners (Griggs and Dunn 1996). Field-dependent learners prefer activities that involve interdependence and cooperation, such as relay races, building puzzles together, following the leader, and collaborative art activities.

Interdependence and cooperation are cultural characteristics that can be found in Latine families (Jalali, 1988). As educators create lesson plans and develop curricula, it is important to emphasize learning activities that promote cooperation, offer a high degree of structure, and allow students to move around freely within a given space.

REFLECTING ON PREFERRED LEARNING STYLES OF DIFFERENT GROUPS

Considering what you now know about the preferred learning styles of African American, Native American, and Latine students, in what ways can you intentionally incorporate the cultures of these students in the overall learning environment?

The Importance of Equitable Learning Environments

The consequences of inequitable learning environments can lead to a sense of inferiority for many students of color. Claude Steele has researched and written extensively on African American students and stereotype threat. Before defining and discussing stereotype threat, let's define stereotypes. According to Sensoy and DiAngelo (2017) *stereotypes* refer to "reduced or simplified characteristics attributed to a group." Stereotypes are dangerous because they paint a very narrow picture of a group and fail to provide the complete story. Stereotypes are misconceptions and give false information about a group of people.

REFLECTING ON STEREOTYPES

✦ What are some common misconceptions about children and families that you have heard in your program?

✦ How can you counter those misconceptions?

When children of color receive messages from educators and society that they are not as intelligent, not as good, or not as capable as their white peers, they ultimately internalize these negative messages. This can result in these children developing a sense of inferiority, illustrated in Claude Steele's work on stereotype threat. *Stereotype threat* is defined as "being at risk of confirming, as self-characteristic, a negative stereotype about one's group" (Steele, 1995). In Steele's research with Black college students, he found that the sheer threat of a stereotype can adversely impact Black students' performance on tests. Steele's research shows that when Black students internalize negative messages about their racial group, their academic performance can be dramatically impaired.

Stereotyping students can be harmful to their sense of identity. For example, Asian American students are often stereotyped as the "model minority" because of the perceived collective success of Asian Americans. Terms such as *smart, hardworking*, and *pleasant* have been used to describe Asian Americans in comparison to other minoritized groups, such as African Americans, who continue to struggle in every aspect of social life. Singham (1998) contends that this idea of Asian Americans as a model minority is rooted in society's ongoing view of Asians as immigrants or foreigners rather than minorities. Attainment of a quality education is an important part of Asian family life (Hwang, 2012); however, the perception of Asian Americans as the "model minority" groups all Asian students together and does not account for any disparities a student may experience. In addition, Teranishi (2015) asserts that this perception is misleading because it presumes that Asian American students do not experience racial inequalities. It is imperative that teachers and directors take the time to get to know each student and family and take care to meet the unique needs of each student.

Creating equitable learning environments for young children includes fostering a positive racial and ethnic identity for young learners. Developing a positive sense of self and identity is a journey for Black, Indigenous, and People of Color (BIPOC) individuals, and this journey starts early in childhood.

York (2016) contends racism impacts the development of children of color in the following ways:

✦ **Overidentification with white people:** The overidentification with white people has its roots in colorism. *Colorism* is the process of discrimination that privileges light-skinned Black people and other people of color over their darker-skinned counterparts (Hunter, 2005). Racism is tied to race and ethnicity, but colorism is uniquely associated with skin tone. Like racism, colorism has its roots in Eurocentrism, slavery, and colonialism. One of the ways slavery was able to thrive in America was through a "divide and conquer" strategy. Slave owners divided enslaved Africans by their skin tone, giving lighter-skinned enslaved people more privileges than those with darker skin. For example, lighter-skinned enslaved people typically worked inside the slave master's house, while darker-skinned enslaved people worked in the fields. Additionally, light-skinned enslaved people were occasionally provided the opportunity to learn to read and write (Davis, 1991). These privileges were given based on the idea that if a person's skin tone was akin to white skin, they were somehow better, smarter, worthier, or more beautiful than dark-skinned individuals. This divide created deep-seated intragroup conflict between dark- and light-skinned enslaved people that transferred through generations and is present in the Black community today. Colorism was prevalent in the infamous "Doll Study" conducted by Kenneth and Mamie Clark in the 1940s. The Clarks found that African American children overwhelmingly selected the white doll to play with as opposed to dolls with skin complexions that were darker. The Clarks concluded that African American children had internalized a racial preference for white dolls, thus suggesting a racial bias toward the African American dolls simply because they had dark skin. Young children may prefer lighter over darker-skinned dolls because they have internalized messages and behaviors that darker skin is somehow "bad" or "ugly."

✦ **Separation and anxiety:** Children of color are less likely to have their cultural experience, identities, and backgrounds affirmed and validated in early learning programs. Their cultural qualities are less likely to be honored and represented in the classroom, creating a sense of isolation. Some children may feel they don't belong or fit in at school (York, 2016). The feeling of isolation can cause young children to disengage from the learning environment.

✦ **Confusion and bewilderment:** Children of color are constantly reminded of their race and/or ethnicity. When they experience racism early in life, they may not fully understand why they are being treated differently or why they are not afforded the same opportunities as white children (York, 2016). For example, during circle story time, the teacher calls on Alex (a white student) who did not have his hand raised and overlooks KeShawn (an African American child) who had his hand raised to answer the question. Children of color too often have to deal with the emotional pain of racism and discrimination, which impairs their sense of self and self-efficacy.

✦ **Feelings of rejection and shame:** Children of color often receive negative messages about who they are from teachers, television, children's books, movies, and so on. They may internalize these messages as they are not good enough, they don't belong, or they are not as smart or as beautiful as white children, resulting in them feeling a sense of inferiority and shame about who they are.

Ebonyse's Experience

I was on a Zoom call with one of my students. The student's three-year-old biracial (African American and white) daughter kept coming near the camera. I could tell she wanted to say hello, but she seemed bashful. I spoke to her every time she was in view of the camera. Her mom finally convinced her to say hi. When she came to speak, she said, "I was too shy to come because my hair is so wild." The girl has big, curly, natural hair. When she said those words, my heart broke. This young girl had already internalized that somehow her hair wasn't beautiful, that she was somehow not good enough and needed to hide from that. At three years old, this girl was already ashamed of her natural curly hair. She had developed a sense of inferiority. I couldn't help but wonder where she got the message that her hair wasn't beautiful.

Conversely, racism impacts white children's development in the following ways:

✦ **Denial of reality:** Often, white people are unaware of the experiences of racism on the mental well-being of people of color. White people never have to think about race in the same way people of color do. In addition, white people often lack exposure to people of color and internalize racist messages about people of color from the media. This creates a false and narrowed narrative about people of color. White people are shielded from the negative effects of racism on people of color, which creates a false sense of reality. Because society continues to deny the realities of racism, many white people believe we're all the same (York, 2016). However, the reality is that race and racism have real consequences on the lives of people of color.

+ **Rigid thinking:** When white people and children are raised in biased environments (York, 2016) and have limited opportunities of exposure to other cultures and other ways of being and doing, they grow up believing that their way of knowing, being, and doing is the only and correct way. This limited thinking reinforces biases and cripples their ability to see the perspectives of other cultures.

+ **Superiority:** According to Roediger (1991), whiteness is viewed as the norm, the standard for universal human values by which all others are viewed and to which they are compared. Whiteness is an ideology that assumes white people are inherently superior and other groups of color are inherently inferior. Because white people hold the collective power, politically, socially, and economically, there is a sense of superiority and domination often internalized by white people. White children can internalize this sense of superiority and may "criticize, ridicule, and reject people of color in order to maintain their own sense of self-worth" (York, 2016).

+ **Fear and hatred:** Just as children of color internalize negative racist messages about who they are, so do white children. In 2007, CNN's Anderson Cooper partnered with a team of child psychologists at the University of Chicago to replicate the Doll Study conducted by the Clarks in the 1940s. In the study, white children also selected the images of darker-skinned children as bad, not pretty or smart, or less likely to be friends. The findings suggest that white children also hold racial biases about children of color. In fact, "by age three or four white children begin to form negative attitudes about people who are different from them, and they develop a high level of rejection of other ethnic groups" (York, 2016). The biases held by white children can influence their interactions with children of color.

✦ The media also plays a significant role in reinforcing the negative biases and misconceptions about people of color. Often people of color are depicted negatively in the media. For example, during Hurricane Katrina, images in the Associated Press showed a young African American male and a white couple wading through and navigating the rising waters. In one image, the white couple had a backpack and an item in their hand. In another image, the African American young man had a garbage bag and an item in his hand. The caption under the image of the African American read, "A young man walks through chest-deep flood water after *looting* [emphasis added] a grocery store..."; the caption under the white couple read, "Two residents wade through chest-deep water after *finding* [emphasis added] bread and soda from a local grocery store" (Kinney, 2005). This illustrates just how entrenched and prevalent implicit racial biases within our society are and how the media can reinforce negative assumptions about a group of people. "White children are socialized to fear people of color" (York, 2016). When white parents and caregivers fail to have honest conversations with their children about race and racism, they perpetuate misconceptions, biases, and false assumptions about people of color. Having authentic conversations about race and racism can mitigate the fear and hatred white children have internalized. The media's reinforcement of negative depictions of people of color exacerbates the fear white people have toward people of color. Challenging and interrupting one's implicit racial biases is one way to reduce fear.

When white children internalize a sense of superiority, they grow up believing they are better than others simply because they are white, which threatens their very humanity. When they lack exposure to people of color, they are unable to empathize with the stress of racism (York, 2016); thus, white children grow up unable to understand the complexities and nuances of racism and the implications it has for people of color.

Although racism impacts white children and children of color, many African American children in particular internalize racial prejudices and often feel a sense of inferiority. Too often African American children are constantly bombarded with daily messages from individuals and institutions that they are not good enough, not as smart, or not as beautiful as white children (White and Wanless, 2019). In school, too, many Black children have experiences that devalue their Blackness, which impact their sense of self and self-esteem.

Crawford and Barbarin (2006) conclude that the stigmatization of preschool Black boys as "bad" or "troublemakers" negatively impacts their self-worth. Teachers persistently mispronouncing the name of a student of color sends the message that the student is not important enough for the teacher to learn the correct pronunciation of their name. Other microaggressions, such as "You are pretty for a Black girl" or "You speak so well," are consistent reminders to Black children and other children of color that they do not belong and are different from the dominant group.

Allen, Scott, and Lewis (2013) assert that racial microaggressions can have a long-term dire effect on the psychological, social-emotional, and intellectual development of students of color. These microaggressions can leave children feeling isolated and excluded. Since many Black children and other children of color internalize racist messages, the adult caregivers in their lives (including teachers) have a responsibility to help them build a positive racial identity as they learn to navigate a racist society. To counter the racist messages that devalue Blackness, many Black families intentionally practice racial socialization to build positive racial identity.

Racial Socialization

Racial socialization has been used to refer to the developmental process by which children acquire specific verbal and nonverbal messages about values, attitudes, behaviors, and beliefs of their racial group (Lesane-Brown, 2006). Racial socialization often includes messages that:

✦ counteract the negative connotations associated with being Black in America,

✦ teach Black children how to navigate a racist society,

✦ demonstrate the racial inequalities in society, and

✦ emphasize racial pride.

Ebonyse's Experience

Growing up in my household, my father routinely had conversations with me about the importance of being proud to be African American. He spoke candidly about the contributions of Africans and African Americans to the world. As a child, I had Black dolls that I played with, and my father celebrated Kwanzaa, an African American holiday observed from December 26 to January 1 that celebrates African American cultural heritage and traditional values.

Other groups of color also practice racial or cultural socialization to instill ethnic and cultural pride in their children. Building a positive racial and ethnic identity with young children is essential for their social-emotional competence.

REFLECTING ON CLASSROOM ACTIVITIES TO PROMOTE RACIAL PRIDE

What classroom activities can you create to instill racial and ethnic pride in young children? How can you foster racial and ethnic pride in the daily life of your classroom?

DIVING DEEPER

Resources to further your understanding of the terms discussed in this chapter:

Ackerman Institute. 2014. *Understanding Social Locations and Identities, Part 1: With Dee Watts-Jones.* Video. https://youtu.be/pSj5xC08eBo

Ackerman Institute. 2014. *Understanding Social Locations and Identities, Part 2: With Dee Watts-Jones.* Video. https://youtu.be/e08Q21HGjio

Ackerman Institute. 2014. *Social Locations and How They Impact Us, Part 3: With Dee Watts-Jones.* Video. https://youtu.be/T-h0gnJes0M

Stereotype Threat: Social Psychology in Action. 2009. Video. https://youtu.be/nGEUVM6QuMg

Stereotype Threat: A Conversation with Claude Steele. 2013. Video. https://youtu.be/failylROnrY

CHAPTER 6

❧ Strengthening Teacher-Child Relationships with Racially and Ethnically Diverse Learners ⤵

Tameka's Experience

During my senior year of college, I had the opportunity to volunteer in a third-grade classroom at one of the local elementary schools. To this day, I consider my time there as one of the most eye-opening experiences I have ever had. In particular, I can recall a conversation with an eight-year-old African American boy named Malik. I had been intentionally partnered with him by Mrs. H, his white female teacher, who advised me to take him out of the room to work with him one on one but also encouraged me not to stress myself out if he did not complete the math assignment that she had provided because he typically did not. It was obvious to me that Malik was not one of the teacher's favorite students. In fact, she considered him to be a problem child, which she communicated in many ways, both verbally and nonverbally. At the time, I really was not sure what to make out of it, but I did not experience Malik in the same way. He seemed loving, happy, and capable, and I looked forward to seeing him each week.

On one particular day, Mrs. H asked me to take Malik to the library to work on a reading assignment. However, in the process of giving me instructions, she also handed me the game Battleship and stated, "If he won't do the worksheet, don't worry about it. Y'all can just play this game." That comment did not sit well with me at all! I felt confused and offended.

It felt as though Mrs. H had already given up on Malik, and I was not okay with that. So I made up my mind that I was going to do everything I could in my time there to prove her wrong about him.

When we got to the library, Malik went straight for the Battleship game. I quickly blocked him from reaching it and let him know that we would play it after we completed the worksheet. He responded, "But Mrs. H said I ain't have to do the worksheet and we can just play the game." I responded by explaining to him how important it was for him to complete his classroom assignments because they were used to assess how much he knew to make sure he was ready for the next grade. I explained that if he never did them, people might assume that he didn't know how and would never know how smart he really was. I ended the conversation with, "I mean, I know how smart you are. I just need you to show everyone else, too." Malik smiled and said, "Okay, Ms. Tameka," and within ten minutes, with very little assistance from me other than a few grammatical corrections, the assignment was complete. I was a bit surprised, not because he completed it but because he did it with such ease. Based on the feedback I had received from Mrs. H, I expected him to struggle, become frustrated, and want to give up, but he displayed the total opposite, which led me to ask, "Malik, why don't you do your work like that in class for Mrs. H?" He responded, "I ain't doing nothing for her, Ms. Tameka. She don't care. She don't even like me." At that moment I felt heaviness in the pit of my stomach followed by increased heat throughout my body. I was heartbroken and angry at the same time. Here was this young Black boy full of potential and ability who had made a conscious decision to disengage from the schooling process, not because he was struggling academically but simply because his teacher failed to take the time to nurture and encourage him.

From that moment, I truly understood the power of positive and nurturing student-teacher relationships. Actually, they are so powerful that the entire trajectory of a person's life can be completely changed simply by their absence or presence.

As I continued to work with Malik, he became more eager to complete his tasks even in my absence, just to show me what he had accomplished when I returned. Each time we would do a celebratory dance to commemorate his success. One day, as I was preparing to leave, Mrs. H pulled me to the side and said, "I don't know what you did to get him to start following directions and do his work, but I appreciate it. I'm really surprised at how much he's changed." I just smiled and responded, "It was always in him. He just needed a little love and encouragement along the way." Although what I said back then was very true, I realize that I could have simply said, "He and I have a good relationship."

REFLECTING ON OUR ASSUMPTIONS ABOUT CHILDREN

Can you think of a time when your assumptions about a child may have hindered you from building a meaningful relationship?

Establishing Meaningful Relationships with Students

The ability to establish meaningful relationships with students is the most powerful and transformative teaching strategy educators need in their pedagogical toolbox. In fact, positive, nurturing relationships can be life changing for both students and their families. Research has consistently shown the connection to positive outcomes in both school engagement and academic achievement (Tobin and Vincent, 2011), and nurturing relationships have been identified as a protective factor from adverse early childhood experiences (Loomis, 2021). The bond between teacher and student sets the tone for classroom interactions and experiences by communicating to the children how the teacher thinks and feels about them, whether positive or negative. Although Tameka was technically not Malik's teacher at the time, the difference in his interactions with Mrs. H and Tameka is a perfect illustration of this statement.

Mrs. H's actions and words conveyed to Malik that he was not valued and, therefore, that his success did not matter, so he did not even try. On the other hand, Tameka's behavior communicated that she valued him, believed in him, and was rooting for his success, so he wanted to do his best.

It is extremely important that young children feel that they matter. When teachers are intentional about creating warm and welcoming environments, children not only feel seen and heard but are assured that their teachers are genuinely concerned about their overall well-being and success (Bakadorova and Raufelder, 2015). These teachers are aware of the individualized needs of their students and are intentional about addressing them. So it's not surprising that high-quality relationships between teachers and students predict better student outcomes, including more positive reading and math achievement, social skills, and class participation (Trang and Hansen, 2020). Furthermore, these types of bonds establish trust, promote open communication, and build community, all of which are particularly important for creating and maintaining culturally sensitive learning environments that embrace the developmental needs of racially and ethnically diverse students. To sustain these types of relationships and environments, educators should be socially and self-aware and should maintain instructional accountability.

Social Awareness

The primary predictors of the quality of teacher-child relationships include gender, race, academic performance, and behavior. In particular, research has shown that children of color are less likely to experience positive interactions but more likely to receive disciplinary referrals than their white peers. This is particularly true when the teacher is representative of a different culture. Additionally, children of color are more likely to be characterized based on negative stereotypes such as "lazy" or "too social" (Trang and Hansen, 2020). In a recent study on the daily discriminatory experiences of Black students in multiple contexts, Devin English and colleagues (2020) found that students reported experiencing an average of five incidents of vicarious or direct discrimination daily, both inside and outside of the school. Unfortunately, this is not happenstance but the remnant of a deep history of institutional and systemic racism and a perpetuation of the cultural conformity within education and society as a whole. It is for this reason that teachers cannot take a color-blind approach to building relationships with a racially and ethnically diverse group of students. All students are *not* the same, and thus they need to be valued and embraced as the unique and multifaceted individuals they are.

Noguera (2008) asserts that establishing these types of relationships is a continuous process in teaching and learning that requires teachers to commit to getting to know about their students in a way that defies stereotypes by building the authentic partnerships discussed in chapter 4. This approach to relationship building ensures that all children are treated as equals and valued as individuals. This is extremely important for students of color because educators can influence the level of protection the students feel and can promote resiliency when they have formed strong bonds. Accordingly, positive interventions at critical moments can neutralize negative external life events that they may experience and lessen the likelihood of negative repercussions from those events (Evans-Winters, 2005). Some examples include a male coach becoming a mentor for a young boy whose father is absent or a teacher making a referral to social services after finding out about a parent or guardian who is experiencing a financial hardship.

The first step in getting to know your students is to understand the sociocultural context in which they live. Accordingly, Boutte and Strickland (2008) suggest that teachers must acknowledge the sociocultural realities of being minorities in the United States and how these realities impact children's schooling experience. In the case of African Americans, Boykin and Toms (1985) describe these realities as a negotiation among three different experiences simultaneously: the mainstream, the minority, and the Black cultural experiences. Each of these experiences possesses its own unique set of requirements that these students must address. The *mainstream experience* refers to adhering to white, middle-class values and personal achievement; the *minority experience* encompasses the recognition of discrimination and the acceptance of being Black; and the *Black cultural experience* addresses racial pride and tradition.

Tameka's Experience

Let me give an example from my own life. In elementary school, my teachers always referred to me as a model student. They emphasized my calm and quiet demeanor and my tendency to keep to myself, all of which are characteristics of mainstream cultural expectations. On the other hand, in the confines of my home, neighborhood, and church, I was loud, vibrant, and expressive. I spoke Ebonics. I was unapologetically me, unapologetically African American, which is rooted in Black culture. Nonetheless, my parents understood the challenges I would face as a Black girl growing up in society where the mainstream experience was predominantly representative of whiteness. They knew the importance of me being able to blend in with my peers in the classroom setting and not giving the teachers any reason to view me as a threat or a problem. It is for this reason that my parents stressed the importance of manners and respect throughout my childhood and obedience in the schooling environment. Consequently, I learned how to efficiently and effectively play the assimilation game at a very early age. There was a time and place for everything, and my parents were active participants in equipping me with the knowledge and skills I needed to better display the appropriate behaviors at the appropriate time.

To help students navigate these realities, Geneva Gay (as cited in Townsend, 2000) recommends that teachers serve as "cultural brokers" who possess the ability to find commonalities between minority and mainstream cultures to use as a basis for classroom practices and interactions. This level of mediation requires teachers to be aware of their own personal biases, to be knowledgeable about the children they serve, and to be able to implement culturally appropriate practices—all of which can be acquired through self-reflection, relationship building, and ongoing intentional professional development.

REFLECTING ON BIAS AND GETTING TO KNOW STUDENTS AND FAMILIES

✦ Can you identify some of the biases you have that could serve as a barrier to effectively meeting the needs of the diverse learners you teach?

✦ What simple activities can you do to intentionally get to know the students and families attached to those biases in an effort to gain greater understanding?

Putting Social Awareness into Practice

It is important to stay knowledgeable about local and national events that may affect your students, either directly or indirectly. By doing so, you can gather insight into changes in behavior and the dispositions and needs of both your students and their families. The best way to begin to identify these issues is by watching the news, conversing with families on a regular basis, and participating in community events.

Tameka's Experience

During my time as a director, we were at the height of civil unrest in our country as a result of repeated police shootings of unarmed Black men. Consequently, outraged citizens of all races and ages were gathering to protest and sometimes riot on a daily basis. Given the fact that my center demographics were around 95 percent Black, I knew that the children and families I served would be impacted. I would engage with the parents during pickup and drop-off about everything that was happening around the country and particularly in our city. Unfortunately, one morning during drop-off, a mother informed me that her brother had been fatally shot during the protest the night before. By having this conversation, I was able to identify what support the family would need at that moment and also establish context for future behaviors and requests over the days to come.

Family Check-Ins

Develop a routine for touching base with your students' families. These check-ins should be used simply to see how they are doing and to find out if there are any family changes or updates that they would like to share with you that might affect their child's classroom performance. You can also use the check-ins to find out if family members need anything from you. These conversations should be very informal and family centered. That means that you should be doing more listening than speaking. It might be a little difficult at first to get the families comfortable enough to talk freely, but with consistency and intentionality you can establish trust, and open communication will likely follow.

Professional Development

Knowledge is power! It is one thing for a teacher to be aware of the social and cultural experiences of their students and families but an entirely different thing to know how to support families going through those experiences. A great way for teachers to increase their skill set is to attend workshops, webinars, and conferences that explicitly address the sociocultural needs of ethnically and culturally diverse children, especially when the presenter represents the cultural group that they are discussing. This is not to say that different cultural groups cannot teach and advocate for other groups, but it is important to acknowledge that there is a unique perspective connected to lived experiences. There is no better person to provide insight on an experience than an individual who has actually experienced it.

> *For example, by now you've noticed that Dr. Mead and I talk very candidly about the Black experience and the corresponding needs of Black children. This is not because other ethnic groups are any less important but because the Black experience is our experience. Hence, we have a particular level of expertise that is intricately woven into who we are, where we come from, and what we've been through. Accordingly, this positions us to educate others on equitable practices for Black children in a way that a white or Latine individual or a member of any other racial or cultural group could not.*

Self-Awareness

Every teacher enters the classroom with their own cultural, racial, and linguistic identities. These identities frame every aspect of their lives, including their attitudes, actions, values, and beliefs. These identities and aspects are also the filters through which and criteria by which we judge others. Terrill and Mark (2000) refer to this notion as teachers being culture-bound, ultimately referring to the way in which their specific cultures frame every aspect of how they show up in their classrooms. The expectations they hold for their students, their perspectives on family engagement, and their assessment of student behaviors are influenced and framed by their cultures. Correspondingly, teachers suggest that being culture-bound is sometimes a limitation on their ability to effectively engage students from a different cultural background. Unfortunately, this concept is most evident in teacher perceptions of appropriate versus inappropriate behaviors. Gregory and Mosely (2013) suggest that student behaviors are often judged based on the cultural norms of their teachers. Each teacher holds their own set of cultural values and beliefs that provide the frame of reference for classroom interaction with students. As a result, students who are most like their teachers tend to be viewed more favorably than those who are not. Such cultural mismatches often result in students being unfairly characterized by popular stereotypes, many of which teachers actually believe and act upon, either consciously or unconsciously.

Whether we realize it or not, each of us has some implicit biases characterized by stereotypical beliefs about a particular group of people that automatically and unconsciously influence the way we judge and interact with people in that group (Gilliam et al., 2016). These biases are directly correlated to characteristics such as race, socioeconomic status, gender, and sexual orientation and determine our perceptions to an extent. Accordingly, those groups we tend to view more positively will be held to higher expectations and are extended more favor; those viewed more negatively are judged more harshly and critically. This explains the overrepresentation of students of color in special-needs programming and the significant disproportionality in the number of suspensions and expulsion of students of color compared to their white peers in K–12 settings dominated by white female educators (Skiba et al., 2011).

It should be noted, however, that implicit bias can be a double-edged sword depending on how an individual chooses to deal with it. On one hand, if an individual refuses to acknowledge and address the existence of biases, they are likely to perpetuate the cycle of discrimination (Gilliam et al., 2016). On the other hand, an individual who acknowledges their biases may overcompensate in their interactions with certain groups. Kunjufu (2002) highlights two attitudes held by white teachers that often lead to them having low expectations for students of color. The first attitude he identifies is the insensitive teacher who makes little effort to relate to Black students. Then there is the liberal teacher who goes to the extreme in trying to compensate for negative risk factors for Black students by lowering expectations and not enforcing boundaries. Although the motivations for these two attitudes differ, the manner in which children of color are perceived in both scenarios is what we call *deficit ideology*. These perceptions often result in inadequate pedagogy driven by low expectations and followed by poor outcomes and negative interactions with students (Trang and Hansen, 2020).

It is for this reason that teachers must have a foundation of racial literacy in which they understand how race and racism shapes the lived experiences of the students and families they serve (Stevenson, 2013). However, the first step in this process is teachers gaining a clear understanding of how their own race affects their daily life and the ways in which it intersects with systems of oppression. This requires reflection. It's very important that all teachers, regardless of culture and economic status, are willing to do honest and in-depth introspection. To become culturally effective and responsive, teachers must be aware of their own personal biases and assumptions. This means getting rid of the façade of being color blind and seeing all children the same, then really owning the thoughts and feelings they hold about the students and families they serve. Here are some of the questions we encourage teachers to consider as they begin to work through this process:

✦ Which students and families do you like to work with the most? the least?

✦ What are the first thoughts you have when you see them?

✦ Where do you think these thoughts come from?

✦ Are these thoughts related to a common stereotype about these groups?

✦ What evidence do you have to affirm that these thoughts about these students and families are valid?

✦ Have you made the effort to get to know the students and their families to better understand who they are in an effort to help shape your feelings and assumptions about them?

It is only when teachers can be critically reflective of their practices that they can begin the work of building nurturing and meaningful relationships that honor the ethnic identity and heritage of their students.

Putting Self-Awareness into Practice

Cultural Autobiography

This is a time for you to tell your story about where you come from, what you've been through, and how it has shaped you into the person that you are today. A quick Google search will lead you to different templates to help you write your cultural autobiography, or you can just do it freestyle. Regardless of which format you choose, you should address the following:

✦ Your cultural identity (values, beliefs, and traditions) and what it means to you

✦ Your experiences with other cultures and how your identity influenced those reactions

- The messages, both positive and negative, you have received about being a member of your particular culture or ethnic group

- The messages, both positive and negative, you have received about those whose cultural backgrounds differ from your own

For this exercise to be effective, it is extremely important that you be honest, specific, and detailed, as your self-reflection will provide critical insight on how your cultural identity could affect how you relate to the students and families you serve. Some of the key details you should look for in your writing are patterns that reveal which cultural groups you tend to favor more and which groups you tend to few more negatively. Once you have identified those patterns, think about your classroom policies and practices, then identify the ways in which the patterns influence your classroom policies and practices. For example, do you find yourself disciplining the groups you have the negative views of more than the others? Do you spend more time engaging with students who are reflective of your more favorable groups?

IMPLICIT BIAS TESTS

There is a wide range of online implicit bias tests that you can take for free. These tests were specifically designed through the collaboration of a group of researchers from various universities who formed a nonprofit organization known as Project Implicit. The purpose of these tests is to help individuals identify biases that they may not even be aware that they hold. Tests can be found at https://implicit.harvard.edu/implicit/takeatest.html

---

Instructional Accountability

Discriminatory practices can emerge in subtle yet powerful ways in the classroom, including in disciplinary practices, teacher expectations, and academic assessments. If teachers are not vigilant and intentional about avoiding such practices, they can sabotage their ability to build trust and establish meaningful relationships with their students (Legette et al., 2020). Hence, it is critical that educators understand that relationship building is an ongoing process that takes consistent reflection and accountability. Just as with any other relationship, teacher-student relationships require work. Educators must be intentional about putting measures in place to safeguard the bonds they have created with their students. Strong teacher-student relationships require a commitment to continued personal and professional growth. In particular, educators must first be willing to:

✦ embrace diversity, be introspective, and have a solid understanding of their own culture;

✦ examine how their culture influences their practices as a teacher, and change any practices that are biased or insensitive; and

✦ find ways to intentionally support and incorporate the cultural identities of their students into the classroom environment.

Next, educators must understand that relationships and instructional practices go hand in hand. As a matter of fact, they are inextricably linked. Both are critical to fostering warm, engaging, and empowering learning environments that can adequately meet the needs of the children in their care. In fact, high-quality instruction and close teacher-child relationships have been identified as the best predictor of academic success for preschoolers (Howes et al., 2008). This speaks volumes about what should be prioritized in our early learning environments. We have to create and maintain culturally affirming learning environments established on trust and collaboration between teacher and student. In other words, we have to be intentional by using teaching practices that focus on student engagement.

Engaged Pedagogy

Engaged pedagogy is about moving beyond theory into practice. In fact, bell hooks (1994) describes engaged pedagogy as a student-centered approach to teaching and learning that creates a space for student voices and experiences to ultimately shape the curriculum. By taking this approach, educators are able to avoid perpetuating classroom practices that value white, middle-class culture at the cost of devaluing all others. Thus, engaged pedagogy dismantles the notion of a one-size-fits-all approaches to curriculum and education. Engaged pedagogy is ever evolving and tailored to the needs, interests, and abilities of the students, and it looks very different from one classroom to the next. This is such a powerful tool for establishing strong relationships, promoting high achievement, and empowering culturally and ethnically diverse children. Engaged pedagogy requires teachers to hold high expectations for their students and requires students to be active participants, both of which help build self-esteem, increase confidence, and improve academic performance (Brophy, 2008). This approach is predicated on an educator's willingness to move beyond academics to the complete well-being of the child. In fact, hooks (1994) asserts that teaching practices must be done in a manner that demonstrates respect and care for the very souls of students.

Tameka's Experience

At my center, engaged pedagogy looked like this:

+ *We recited a daily affirmation to remind the children that they are important, amazing, and enough, simply by being who they are and regardless of what anyone else has to say. This was our way of countering the impact of the many media images of negative stereotypes of Black people to which they had already been exposed.*

+ *We exposed young children to positive, scholarly role models related to each theme of study and representative of their own racial and cultural backgrounds, life experiences, and interests to make the curriculum more meaningful and to reinforce the fact that they can achieve the same level of greatness and success. For example, we talked about Ruby Bridges, the first Black child to integrate an all-white school in the United States, and the courage it took for her to walk into the school in spite of being treated so meanly by others. We gave the students the opportunity to express their thoughts and feelings about what they had learned by reenacting Ruby Bridges's experience, writing and illustrating stories about a time they were courageous, and making up songs and chants about being brave.*

+ *We used the "What I know, What I want to know, What I learned" (commonly called KWL) chart to actively engage students in the planning process. This is a simple process that first starts with discussing and documenting what students already know and what they would like to know about a topic. Teachers then create activities and experiences that provide the knowledge that the students desire to gain. Finally, teachers have a follow-up conversation with their students after the implementation of those lessons to determine what they learned from them.*

Through each of these experiences, our students felt like valued members of our learning community while being empowered both collectively and individually. As a result, we observed an increase in confidence and the willingness to take chances and try new things. It was uplifting to see children who would not normally choose to be the center of attention out of fear and shyness eagerly volunteering to take the lead in various activities and opportunities.

REFLECTING ON THE NEEDS OF DIVERSE LEARNERS

✦ How would you rate your willingness to revise your current teaching strategies to intentionally accommodate the needs of diverse learners?

✦ If you are not willing to do this yet, what are the barriers and how might they impact your effectiveness as an educator?

Putting Instructional Accountability into Practice

Reflective Journaling

Journaling is an easy way for educators to capture their thoughts, feelings, and experiences at a specific moment in time. It also provides invaluable data on what is occurring in the classroom, which will help teachers identify issues, challenges, and changes that need to be made. The things you should consider addressing in your journaling are things that are going well, things that are not going well, times you may have been biased, and any questionable or challenging interactions you've had with students or their families. The great thing about journaling is that it is completely private, unless you choose to share, so there is no fear of repercussions for honesty. It's a great way to keep yourself accountable.

Professional Learning Communities

Your colleagues can serve as an additional measure of accountability for your instructional practices. There is value in getting unbiased feedback. There are many things we say and do that we're not aware of until someone else brings it to our attention. We encourage you to have a trusted colleague review your lesson plans, conduct an observation, or even talk through a challenging situation. In particular, we recommend finding colleagues who are culturally different from you that possess a different level of insight. Use their feedback to enhance and revise your practices.

Difficult Conversations

As early education practitioners, it is imperative that we are able to engage in conversations about culture and race. Much like religion and politics, these are topics that most people try to stay away from by any means necessary. Conversations about them are often uncomfortable, as they evoke a variety of thoughts and feelings that we would prefer not to address. However, it is not until we are willing to be open and honest in such discussions that we can begin to unpack and heal cultural and racial trauma, both as individuals and as society as a whole. It is critical that we not only understand our own cultural identity but also understand what that means in relation to our interactions with others. For example, does our identity place us in positions of power and privilege, or does it position us to be marginalized and discriminated against? These conversations should happen both informally (for example, through random conversations with your colleagues or people in the community) and formally (through interactions such as organized conversations in professional learning communities or community meetings).

Equity/Anti-Bias Checklist

Checklists are an objective measure for determining whether you are creating equitable and unbiased learning environments for your students. You can find several online, but we recommend you review *Anti-Bias Education for Young Children and Ourselves* by Louise Derman-Sparks and Julie Olsen Edwards, as well as the position statement of the National Association for the Education of Young Children (NAEYC) on advancing equity in early childhood, to help you create your own checklist that is specifically tailored to your classroom.

REFLECTING ON INSTRUCTIONAL ACCOUNTABILITY

✦ What difficult conversations need to be had in your program?

✦ What strategies are currently in place for administration and staff to hold each other accountable? If none, what are some that could be added?

CHAPTER 7

Improving Instructional Practices with Racially and Ethnically Diverse Learners

"Setting a goal is not the main thing. It is deciding how you will go about achieving it and staying with that plan."

—Tom Landry, professional football player and coach

Establish a Plan

Although the notion of equity is not new to the field of early childhood education, it has become a popular buzzword in educational circles when discussing the needs of ethnically diverse and historically marginalized children of color. In fact, it has come to the forefront of many state and national policy agendas, resulting in the development of several position statements and policy briefs on providing equitable early learning experiences for young children and their families.

Nonetheless, there still remains an obvious disconnect between embracing equity as a goal and actually implementing it as a practice. The reality is that, although setting a goal for advancing equity is a necessary first step, alone it is simply not enough. Creating an inclusive and equitable classroom environment requires intentional planning by both administrators and teachers and necessitates a thorough understanding of the student population and their families, a unified vision of equity, and a shared commitment to consistently implement practices and strategies. A simple approach to this level of intentional planning is simply being in the know. In particular, know those you are serving, know what you believe, and know that implementation is a marathon and not a sprint!

Know Whom You Are Serving

Improving instructional practices for racially and ethnically diverse students requires teachers to be intentional in planning their lessons and curriculum to ensure they are infusing students' cultural aspects into the learning environment. Intentional planning requires teachers to be keenly aware of their cultural identity and social location, as well as the cultural identities and social locations of their students, and to have a thorough understanding that children exist within the context of their families and communities.

Culture is central to how we identify ourselves, our perceptions of the world and how we navigate it, and the values and beliefs that shape and guide our lives. Because culture is central to our identity, it is critically important for educators to understand the role social location not only plays in our work with young children but also in our pedagogical practices and approaches. The concept of *social location* was introduced earlier in the text and, simply stated, refers to the ways in which one's various identities (race, gender, social class, geographic location, religion, ability, age, sexual orientation) impact how we are generally perceived by others in society as a whole. It determines the privileges we are afforded, the discrimination we face, and the opportunities we receive. Consequently, teachers need to:

✦ **understand how the differing aspects of their identities place them in positions of power and privilege.** For example, a white, middle-class, female teacher must understand that being a member of the dominant cultural group has allowed her to access resources and opportunities that may not be afforded to the students and families she serves who are from lower socioeconomic backgrounds.

✦ **understand how their power and privilege influence their values and beliefs about teaching and learning, and how these values and beliefs are demonstrated in their classroom environments.** For example, a teacher who grew up in a home with computer and internet access and college-educated parents may be more likely to provide lots of family engagement activities that require the use of technology, with the assumption that all families have the same resources, knowledge, and abilities that her family had.

✦ **understand how the differing aspects of their student's identities, especially those of students who are racially and ethnically diverse, influence their life experiences, opportunities, and outcomes, and how those things are similar and different from their own.** For example, a white, middle-class teacher must recognize and understand that their Black students from low-income households are likely to encounter acts of discrimination and prejudice that they never will. Thus, the teacher becomes intentional about making their classroom a safe space that promotes a sense of belonging and community for all.

These understandings are vital for building authentic relationships between teachers and families. These relationships are key in preventing teachers from making assumptions, generalizations, or oversimplifications about their students and their families. When teachers understand who their students are, where they come from, and the challenges they face, teachers can better meet students' unique needs. For example, an ill-informed teacher may problematically generalize the needs of all their Latine students because of their shared Hispanic background, without realizing a Latine immigrant student's needs are quite different from those of a native-born Latine student. The teacher may thus fail to provide the level of support and instruction that the students truly need.

Greater understanding leads to greater appreciation of the cultural backgrounds and lived experiences of the students and families we serve. Additionally, it sets the stage for a classroom that is both inclusive and welcoming. It is imperative that students feel seen and heard in the classroom environment through the literature that teachers read, the images that they display, and the activities that they engage in on a regular basis.

REFLECTING ON SOCIAL LOCATION

✦ What are the key characteristics that make up your identity?

✦ How do those characteristics privilege or disadvantage you?

✦ How do those characteristics compare to those of the students in your care?

Culturally and structurally diverse families are the new normal in many early childhood programs. These include families across various racial and ethnic backgrounds, as well as immigrant and refugee families. In addition to the diversity of families across different cultures, family structures have evolved over time. While the nuclear family is still very common, other family compositions, including single-parent, blended, same-sex, grandparent caregivers, and extended families, are equally as common. Other types of families include foster, adoptive, and military, as well as families with incarcerated loved ones. Children do not exist in a vacuum. Their family (caregivers) play such an integral part in their development that it is paramount for teachers to build trusting, authentic relationships with families.

Developing trusting relationships with families requires teachers and early childhood leaders to become culturally responsive by understanding their own culture and social location, examining and challenging their personal biases, and developing engagement strategies that are conducive to families' cultural backgrounds. While examining their personal biases is important, teachers must learn to acknowledge the strengths of all families in spite of any adversity the family is experiencing. Many young children have experienced some form of trauma, such as child abuse or neglect, community violence, or poverty. It is necessary for teachers to acknowledge that not all families experiencing trauma lack resilience. As a family-service practitioner with more than eighteen years of experience working with children and families, I (Ebonyse) have learned that many families experiencing trauma are not only resilient but also resourceful. These families have learned to utilize their strengths as resources to ensure the well-being of their families.

Teachers must learn to view families from a strengths-based lens rather than a deficit lens. This is especially important for racially and ethnically diverse families, since many of these families may already feel isolated, marginalized, and disengaged from early childhood programs. Too often these families are criticized for not engaging in a program the way teachers expect families to be engaged. It is critical for teachers to acknowledge the unique strengths of each family, respect the cultural values and beliefs that guide their parenting practices, and honor the family's funds of knowledge that sustain their family well-being.

Putting a Strengths-Based Approach into Practice

"All about Our Family" Survey

Develop and distribute a family survey. Make sure to ask questions that will encourage the families to think more deeply about themselves while allowing you to get to know them at a deeper level. Possible survey items include the following:

✦ Describe your family's culture in three words.

✦ What makes your family unique?

✦ If each family member could have a superpower, what would it be, and why?

These types of questions are a less-intrusive technique of encouraging families to communicate openly and honestly. You can provide such surveys in both virtual and hard-copy formats and have them translated for each of the languages represented in your program.

Family Treasure Chest

Ask each family to decorate a shoebox to create their very own family treasure chest. Instruct them to decorate the outside of their box with pictures and words that describe their family and to place inside the box representations of things their family treasures or likes the most, such as hobbies, traditions, music, foods, and stories. In consideration of various family resources, make sure to collect extra shoeboxes, markers, crayons, construction paper, glue sticks, scissors, magazines, scissors, stickers, and any other crafting supplies to send home with students as needed. Invite parents to come in and do show-and-tell with their child about their treasure chest or send in audio or a written description of their chest for the teacher to support the student in sharing on their behalf.

Know What You Believe and Why

To create and sustain equitable early learning environments, a cohesive understanding of what equity means—particularly as it relates to the children and families you serve—is necessary. All educators must have the conviction that each and every child deserves high-quality early care and education regardless of who they are or where they come from, and educators must have a commitment to meet children's developmental needs by any means necessary. This requires educators to view each child as an individual and member of their cultural group, while simultaneously recognizing the child as an invaluable member of the classroom community. It also requires educators to be active participants in dismantling traditional structures of power and privilege in the classroom environment that position white children for success but create barriers for children of color. It is impossible to achieve this without addressing the issue of race—any attempt to take a color-blind approach is a denial of the existence of systemic inequalities and a perpetuation of institutional racism within early childhood education. Darling-Hammond (2005) emphasizes that, unless systemic inequities are acknowledged and addressed, educational policies will continue to fail students of color by identifying the students as the cause of their own failure. For many educators, this type of approach will be uncomfortable and challenging, as it contradicts their own early education experiences, teacher-education training, and even personal beliefs, which is why it is so important for administrators to lead their educators in developing a unified vision for their programs.

Program administrators are instrumental in establishing a culture of equity and inclusion in early learning programs. They must ensure that the cultural and developmental needs of the children enrolled in their programs are met and that their teachers are adequately prepared to effectively implement the necessary curriculum and strategies. Thus, administrators must start with a clear and specific statement of the mission, vision, and values of the program. Although it is the responsibility of the administrator to lead this effort, its development should be a collaborative effort among stakeholders: teachers, parents, community partners, and so on. It is important for all stakeholders to feel invested in the process of advancing equity.

REFLECTING ON EQUITY

✦ How do you define *equity*?

✦ How does your understanding of equity differ from your understanding of equality?

In the development of your statement of the mission, vision, and values of the program, the following are a few questions to consider:

✦ What is the message you want to convey about your program's commitment to educate and empower culturally and ethnically diverse learners? How will you convey this message to families? school staff? the community?

✦ What are your beliefs and convictions about equity that fuel that commitment?

✦ How will you know that your program is successfully creating an equitable and inclusive early learning environment for all learners?

✦ What resources and supports do you have in place to sustain your commitment to equity?

By answering these questions, you will be able to set a blueprint for equity to guide your program as you move forward. However, keep in mind that this should be a working document that evolves as your program evolves. It should also be a document that is used to inform the policies and practices that govern your center moving forward, including everything from curriculum to enrollment and staffing. This is particularly important for staffing, as the teachers will be on the front lines in the creation and maintenance of equitable learning environments for the children in their care.

NAEYC (2019) developed a position statement entitled *Advancing Equity in Early Childhood Education* that addresses the roles of both the early childhood administrator and the classroom educator in creating equitable learning environments. In fact, the statement provides specific recommendations of strategies, activities, and practices that can be easily used to develop a strong equity statement for any early learning environment. We strongly encourage you to review this document to guide the development of your equity statement. You can find it at https://www.naeyc.org/resources/position-statements/equity

A well-written equity statement will provide teachers with insight into their role in ensuring equitable outcomes as well as position them to make informed decisions about whether the program is still a good fit for them.

This is a difficult yet necessary part of the process for creating inclusive and equitable early learning environments for all children because uncommitted teachers will only serve as hindrances to the work that is being done. Accordingly, this statement should also be incorporated into the interviewing and onboarding process for new teachers to ensure that they share the same values and beliefs about equity.

Equity Advisory Board

Identify three to five stakeholders who are representative or directly connected to the cultural backgrounds and developmental needs of the children in your care to serve on an advisory board for your program. The purpose of this board is to provide expertise in developing equitable policies and practices for the children and families you serve.

Equity Commitment Agreement

Drawing from your equity statement, develop a commitment agreement for each teacher to sign. This will not only ensure that each teacher understands their responsibilities but will also help hold them accountable for fulfilling them. These agreements can be added to staff files as official paperwork.

Know That Implementation Is a Marathon and Not a Sprint

A commitment to equity is a courageous call to action. It requires a great deal of self-reflection and intentionality as you determine how your program reinforces or contradicts notions of equity and inclusion. Each administrator and teacher must be willing to interrogate their own values, beliefs, and practices and to address each issue as it arises. Some of these issues may be addressed quickly, while others may take a little longer, particularly regarding the shifting of mindsets and the deconstruction of normative standards of early care and education.

Unfortunately, many teachers, although well intentioned, confuse the notion of equity with equality, believing that as long as they are treating everyone equally, they are meeting each child's developmental needs. Perhaps the problem lies in the fact that the policies and practices that govern the early childhood education field are often based on a one-size-fits-all framework. This framework operates under the assumption that all children should develop according to Eurocentric norms (Boutte, 2012), completely ignoring the influence that culture has on growth and development. In fact, many teachers feel that teaching is somehow culturally neutral and thus do not feel it necessary to alter their teaching styles or adjust their expectations.

Consequently, emphasis is often placed on implementing developmentally appropriate practices; culture becomes relegated to the celebration of diversity. Hence, teachers engage in a checklist of superficial practices, such as providing multicultural toys for children, acknowledging special holidays, and placing pictures of people from different ethnic groups around the room. Such practices are simply not enough. True equity requires teachers to be willing to accept their role in perpetuating inequities in the classroom and to be prepared to adapt to new ways of thinking and teaching.

It is commonly said that it takes about twenty-one days on average to form a new habit, but the reality is that there is no such magic number, especially for complex behaviors. It will likely actually take much longer. Habit building is a process that will come with its share of challenges. For some, the process will be uncomfortable and frustrating, as it will require them to go against what they would typically think and how they would normally behave. That said, it is important for administrators and teachers to give themselves and each other grace. The process of becoming equity minded is a journey through which we are all starting at different levels of understanding and readiness. That means some will progress and adjust quickly, while others will need a lot more support. However, many will push through this discomfort and emerge as invaluable partners in advancing equity in the program. As long as everyone remains committed to seeing the journey through, change will be inevitable.

How Administrators Can Put a Commitment to Equity into Practice

Short-Term Goals

Establish short-term goals that build upon the teachers' strengths. These goals should be realistic and easily attainable in a short period of time. For example, teachers can enhance their classroom environment by ensuring that each and every child sees themselves reflected in classroom materials and displays.

Check-Ins

Schedule regular check-ins to discuss how the process is going. This will encourage communication and establish supportive connections among staff, which are vital to the success and sustainability of equity within the program.

Set the Stage: Preparing the Learning Environment

Once you establish a plan, it is now time to set the stage for action. It is time to prepare your learning environment to reflect the cultural, linguistic, and social identities of the children and the families whom you serve. This is a very powerful and necessary first step in the process because it welcomes them into the space, affirms their identities, and fosters their sense of belonging. Creating this type of environment for

> **"The walls of a school should reflect future possibilities. The hall should honor dreams. The rooms to help prepare them."**
> —Heather Wolpert-Gawron, middle-school teacher and coach

the children and families you serve helps reassure parents that their children are in good hands and helps children feel safe and secure, physically and emotionally. Safety and security are paramount to children's academic success. When children feel this level of comfort, they are able to confidently explore their learning environment without reservation. There are several strategies that early learning programs can use to set the stage for diverse learners, including the use of wall displays, books, toys, and instructional materials that promote equity and inclusion throughout the program. Additionally, administrators must ensure that all educators have professional-development opportunities addressing the role of culture in creating equitable learning environments and promoting family engagement.

Displays, Toys, and Instructional Materials

The appearance of the physical environment is the first impression your program will make on children and families. In fact, what they see and hear sends messages about who and what your program values. Take a moment and look at the pictures hanging on the walls in the lobby, hallways, and classrooms. Who and what do you see? Who is missing? Are all families reflected in these displays? Likewise, these questions should be asked about the instructional and play materials in the classroom. More often than not, the answer to these questions will affirm some groups while unintentionally excluding others. For example, a program may have several displays of families that capture two-parent households but none that reflect the single-parent or same-sex parents they also serve. Although subtle, these types of situations convey powerful messages that in some cases have long-lasting effects. For this reason, any educators committed to promoting equity must critically examine all of their program's displays and materials. To avoid issues of bias and exclusion in your environment, here are a few things you should look for:

✦ Opportunities to display photographs of the children and families you serve inside and outside of the program, such as pictures of the children showing different emotions to make a poster about feelings or family photos to make a family tree in the classroom

✦ Instructional and play materials with realistic images that depict the represented groups in various roles and professions, particularly those that they may not commonly be presented in, such as a Black man working as an early childhood teacher or a Latina woman working as a lawyer

✦ Instructional and play materials written and recorded in the home languages of the various cultural and ethnic groups of the children and families you serve

✦ Art materials and play materials that represent the various skin tones of the children

✦ Books in which the main characters are positively portrayed and culturally similar, have familiar life experiences, or emphasize prominent members of the cultural communities of the children

Incorporating these types of materials counters negative stereotypes while promoting cultural pride, which are critical to creating equitable and inclusive high-quality early learning programs. Although beneficial for all children, this is exceptionally important for children of color. They are constantly receiving messages, both directly and indirectly, through mainstream cultural and societal practices about who they are and where they come from. Actually, by the time Black children enter kindergarten, they have already been exposed to an abundance of media images depicting negative stereotypes about themselves and their communities. Unfortunately, these messages are often reinforced by school resources such as books and curricula. Children's literature often portrays African Americans negatively, and this may be overlooked by most readers because of the assumed innocence of children's books. For example, Black children are often characterized as the class clown or the mischievous sidekick implemented as comic relief. The perpetuation of such negative stereotypes can have detrimental effects on the psyches of Black children by negatively impacting their motivation, engagement, and academic achievement (Seaton, 2010). Consequently, it is important for teachers to confront social injustices and negative perceptions of their students of color instead of pretending they do not exist.

Professional-Development Opportunities

Equipping teachers with knowledge and skills to effectively address these issues is the next step in setting the stage. Unfortunately, although it is highly likely that most early educators want to meet the developmental needs of each child in their classrooms, the reality is that many simply do not know what to do or where to start. A great place to begin is by checking with your local resource and referral agency to see if they are providing any training on equity or bias or have any recommendations for trainers who specialize in equity and anti-bias work. Your local institutions of higher education may be a great resource as well, as they may have early childhood faculty whose research focus is on equity and inclusion who would be willing to serve as an educational consultant for your program. Additionally, there is an abundance of literature on the subject that can aid in professional development; some of our favorites are included on page 120. Make sure that the resources and support you select go beyond just celebrating differences (typically the focus of diversity work) to a focus on understanding the dynamics of power and privilege and identifying teaching practices that can address them in the early childhood setting.

Consider working on the following topics:

✦ Implicit bias

✦ Culture as a teaching strategy (culturally responsive teaching, culturally sustaining pedagogy, and so on)

✦ Family engagement for ethnically diverse families

✦ Authentic strengths-based assessments

✦ Multilingualism

✦ Positive guidance and limit-setting

✦ Inclusive practices for children with exceptionalities

Although not exhaustive, this list covers a variety of topics that are relevant to issues of equity in early childhood. Knowledge gained from these types of workshops will assist early educators in supporting the needs of diverse children and their families.

Promoting Family Engagement

Family engagement is not only essential to the development of young children, but it has also been identified as a key protective factor that helps to minimize the impact of negative experiences for low-income ethnic-minority children (McWayne et al., 2013). Partnerships between families and programs help bridge the gap between home and school, making for a much smoother transition.

For many young children, the transition process between home and school is both challenging and overwhelming because the difference between their home culture and school culture is great. Families can be invaluable resources in making learning meaningful for their children. That said, it is important to keep families informed about the goals and intentions of the program and to intentionally preplan potential family engagement opportunities.

REFLECTING ON ASSUMPTIONS ABOUT FAMILIES

+ What perceptions or assumptions do you hold about the families in your program that have a different cultural, linguistic, family composition, or socioeconomic background than you?

+ How do you think your perceptions or assumptions might affect your relationships with these families?

Putting Family Engagement into Practice

Family Town Halls

Conduct family town halls quarterly, both virtually and in person, to accommodate families' various needs. This is a time to review program policies and goals, address parent concerns, and receive parent feedback.

Family Surveys

Conduct surveys on the parents' and guardians' hopes and dreams for their children, as well as their talents, special skills, and occupations. This information can be used to plan parent-engagement opportunities. For example, families and caregivers can be invited to share a talent or teach a special skill related to a unit of study. This not only encourages engagement but also makes families and caregivers feel like valued members in the learning process.

Family Leadership

Establishing families as advocates and leaders is one of the family outcomes of the *Head Start Parent, Family, and Community Engagement Framework* (2018). Families and caregivers are the experts on their children and can serve in leadership and advocacy roles that benefit not only their own children but the overall child-care community. Invite families and caregivers to serve on child-care boards, to speak at state and national conferences, to join a professional child-care organization, or to establish a family advisory committee at the center. Families serving in leadership roles are more likely to be engaged in child-care centers because they feel welcomed, empowered, and valued. When family members and caregivers can serve in leadership roles that include them in decision-making about program policy and their children's learning and development, they know they are respected and recognized as invaluable resources in the child-care center.

Family Engagement Projects

Identify at least two simple projects related to the curriculum that families and caregivers can work on together with students and send to the center for display. The projects can be displayed in the lobby or in individual classrooms. If possible, each display should be accompanied by a photo of the family and a fun fact. This will allow the educator to learn more about their students' families while simultaneously allowing the families in the program to learn more about each other.

Take Action

Now that you have a plan, it is time to do the work. Good intentions are meaningless without corresponding actions. Change is not always easy; in fact, it can be overwhelming and hard to visualize without concrete examples. Although working toward equity in early childhood is not a new concept, it can still feel rather

"Action always beats intention!"
—Unknown

ambiguous. Sometimes it helps to see and hear about the experiences of others as a frame of reference for what to do and where to start. Following is a vignette of Tameka's own experiences when creating an equitable and inclusive early learning environment as a program administrator of an urban early childhood program.

Establishing a Plan: Tameka's Experience

My center was strategically located in a high-needs African American community. Although we served families from a variety of backgrounds and socioeconomic statuses, most were African Americans living at or below the poverty line. The children were those traditionally labeled "at risk" for academic failure. Stepping into the role, I was well aware of the challenges associated with these circumstances and wanted to be intentional about partnering with staff and families to minimize the effects of the circumstances as much as possible, particularly as they related to meeting the developmental needs of each child. Because the center was purposely built to provide high-quality care to underserved populations, it was well-funded and had an abundance of resources, including family-support services, therapeutic services, and access to onsite professional development and technical assistance for our teachers. I was confident that the children were going to be well-equipped for success and would receive the same high-quality education as their white peers in more affluent neighborhoods. As a matter of fact, we had everything a program could possibly need to meet the needs of ethnically diverse children and families. Or so I thought. I soon realized that equity in resources does not always equate to equity in experiences, nor does it prevent issues of implicit bias or deficit thinking. Unfortunately, within my first few months as a new director, I encountered both issues. Although there were many incidents that highlighted these issues, two primary incidents come to mind.

The first involved the marketing of the program. One of my priority responsibilities was to assist in giving tours and discussing our program with potential donors. After conducting a few of these presentations, I noticed that the financial hardships and corresponding life circumstances of our families were often used as a marketing strategy by the parent organization to solicit donations and additional funding.

Although this strategy was often effective, I found it to be quite problematic, as it was a gross mischaracterization of the children and families that we served. Many of our families were not financially wealthy, but they were unquestionably prosperous in other ways. They brought a wealth of knowledge, skills, and abilities to our center. They were involved, present, and always willing to help, and I was determined to make sure that they would be recognized and valued as such.

The second incident involved an interaction with a white parent of one of the two-year-olds enrolled, who was concerned that our partnership with Head Start, a federally funded preschool program specifically designed to promote school readiness for low-income children, was negatively affecting the quality of our program. According to this parent, the center had changed too much since partnering with Head Start, with the classes becoming bigger and the behavior of the children seemingly becoming worse. She further asserted that the problem was that the children were seeing violence in their homes and neighborhoods and then turning around and bringing those behaviors into the classroom. She felt that the situation was ultimately affecting her son and the other children who were not accustomed to such behavior, which was unfair.

Several factors made her statements problematic. First, this concern stemmed from the fact that her son had been bitten several times by one of his Black classmates, which is typical behavior in a two-year-old classroom rather than a violent act intentionally inflicted upon her child. Second, she assumed the classmate was a part of the Head Start program because he was Black, when in fact there was not a single Head Start student in her child's classroom. Lastly, she assumed that students receiving Head Start funding came from violent households, which made me question which characteristics of Head Start students she was using to form her assumptions. Was it low socioeconomic status? Was it race? Were these characteristics synonymous to her?

As a result of these experiences, I knew that for my program to advance equity I needed to change the narratives of deficit ideology concerning African Americans, not only for the children but for the parents as well. The beliefs that African American children are inherently inferior and can be characterized by popular stereotypes would not be permitted in my program. I felt responsible for ensuring that the center would be a safe place for each and every child. Even if they did not feel valued and celebrated anywhere else, they would at my program!

From my own experiences and educational background, I understood that traditional approaches to education would not suffice in the creation of this uplifting, culturally affirming counternarrative and that I had to be willing to do something different. As always, I worked to tailor the early learning experiences within my program to meet the cultural needs of the children and families I served.

As I took some time to observe my center in action, I noticed a natural ebb and flow in the daily interactions between students, families, and staff. It was unscripted, unplanned, and authentic. We spoke the same language. We related to each other's success and struggles. We shared a common culture. Each day, we showed up, simply being ourselves. Nothing was forced, and connections were natural. This was a collective experience with shared meaning, and it belonged to all of us. It unified us. Next, I spent some time conversing with parents about their hopes and dreams for their children and realized that common goals included school readiness and character development. I also realized that, although we had an abundance of resources, we had very few materials that highlighted or illustrated people of color. I wanted to be sure I addressed all of these issues in our program.

Thus, I identified four guiding principles:

1. *Fostering a school culture of unity and respect*

2. *Studying scholars whose cultures reflect those of the teachers and students represented in the program*

3. *Emphasizing school readiness through reinforcing essential academic skills such as emergent literacy and mathematics*

4. *Including character education to equip the students with skills and traits to positively engage in social interactions with others*

5. *These guiding principles would inform both our curriculum and practices from then on.*

The first step I took was to meet with a bookseller who specialized in children's literature. I told her my goals and gave her the demographics of the students in my center. She provided a list of books that reflected the children's cultures and life experiences and taught valuable lessons. I ordered a couple of books for each classroom. Next, I did an online search of several early learning companies to find culturally inclusive materials and ordered dolls, puzzles, art materials, dramatic play materials, and games that reflected the backgrounds of the students in my classroom. Finally, my teachers took photographs of the children engaging in various activities throughout the center and added them to the classroom displays. The teachers also asked parents to create family posters highlighting family interests, and they put these up to display as well.

Once the environment was set, I wanted to make sure that my teachers felt confident in using the cultures of their students for more effective teaching, so I planned a series of professional development activities over the course of a few months in lieu of our monthly staff meetings. During the first activity, I guided my teachers through self-reflection exercises to make sure they had an understanding of their own cultural biases and the potential impact of such biases on their teaching practices. One such exercise required them to identify common stereotypes about the families we served, their thoughts about those stereotypes, and how such thoughts could possibly affect their classroom practices and interactions. This activity led to some rich discussion about the existence of implicit bias, the dangers of color-blind ideology, and the importance of actively countering both.

Next, we examined several research studies and news articles on the effects of cultural identity on classroom dynamics and educational inequities. Then we viewed *The Unequal Opportunity Race*, a short film that uses the analogy of a relay race to illustrate how obstacles such as wealth disparities, discrimination, and inequitable schooling experiences hinder the social, academic, and economic advancement of African Americans (Pinto, 2010). The video had a powerful impact and generated the type of vulnerable and candid conversations early educators must have to authentically create equitable and inclusive early learning environments for children of color.

Finally, I introduced the concept of culturally sustainable pedagogy to the staff. We talked about the role of culture in development. I highlighted the ways in which the children's culture can bridge the gap between home and school, such as using their home language to help them understand standard English or using music with melodies and rhythms similar to those in the music they listen to in the home environment. Additionally, we discussed the importance of developing cultural pride and scholarly identity in our students to affirm that they are capable of great accomplishments. After discussing these things, I provided the teachers with an initial lesson plan, and we began to brainstorm additional activities as a group. At the end of these sessions, the teachers not only walked away with a greater understanding of equity, but they also had a toolbox of resources and activities to embed into their classroom environments.

We decided to introduce these new guiding principles to our families through our summer enrichment program because the summers allow for more flexibility, which is essential for the implementation of new practices. To build on the culture of unity already established throughout our program, we started with a morning assembly. This assembly was a time when we all gathered and set the tone for the day. During this time, we recited an affirmation, sang songs, and repeated chants that affirmed children's strengths and brilliance as young scholars. The music and chants reflected the rhythm and beats that children were accustomed to in their home environments, which made them easy for the children to learn. Although the assembly was initially led by the teachers, the students soon took over. They were not just participating, they were fully engaged and having fun.

This same excitement carried over into each of the classrooms as the teachers highlighted both prominent and overlooked scholars who reflected the cultures of our students and had made significant contributions to our world. This was a necessary component because exposing young children to positive scholarly role models who represent their own racial and cultural backgrounds allows them to make a personal connection. Furthermore, discussions about these scholars not only exposed the children to the richness of their past but also gave them a glimpse of multiple possibilities for their future (Akua, 2020). Additionally, to support character education, the teachers introduced the students to a specific character trait that connected to each cultural scholar. For the children this not only introduced and reinforced positive character traits, but it also gave them a visual of that trait in action. For example, when we discussed Ruby Bridges, the first Black child to integrate an all-white school in the United States, we focused on courage. We defined courage as doing something even when it frightens you, particularly if it is something that will help yourself or others. Furthermore, we emphasized the fact that being courageous and doing what is right may require you to do things by yourself and that there is an inner strength that we are given to help us to do it.

REFLECTING ON PUTTING EQUITY INTO PRACTICE

✦ What are some guiding principles that would adequately and equitably address the learning and development needs of the students in your program?

✦ What steps would you need to take to ensure that your program is fully equipped to implement them?

CHAPTER 8

Revising and Creating Equitable Policies and Practices

To fully address the needs of racially and ethnically diverse students, administrators and early educators must be willing to examine the context surrounding the policies and practices attached to traditional early childhood frameworks. In particular, we must scrutinize the sociopolitical climate, knowledge base, and belief systems associated with them. We can start by asking questions such as the following:

✦ What was the state of early childhood education at the time the policy or practice was developed, and who was in leadership?

✦ What were the pervasive understandings of child development?

✦ Whose were the prevailing voices?

✦ Whose were the missing voices, and most importantly, why they were excluded?

It is not until we are able to answer these types of questions that we can begin to effectively evaluate whether our practices and policies are truly equitable. This may require you to do a little research, but it is necessary to understand why policies are problematic before you can evaluate them and make the appropriate revisions.

Unfortunately, the truth of the matter is that, throughout our country's history, various policies and practices have been strategically implemented to privilege some and marginalize others. For example, let's consider the issue of segregation. Even after the 1954 *Brown v. Board of Education* ruling that banned segregated schools, the strategic separation of various racial and ethnic groups persists within many schools today. This is not a coincidence but the result of intentional practices, such as rezoning school districts and the enforcement of "neighborhood schools" under the guise of promoting student success, preventing overcrowding, and preserving a sense of community. Although there may be some merit to these explanations, they are also part of a more deceptive strategy for controlling the cultural demographics of the student population in certain areas.

Neighborhoods are primarily segregated by income, and if school districts are zoned accordingly, it is inevitable that the schools will be as well. Furthermore, if we take it a step further and look at the correlation between socioeconomic status and race, we see an additional level of segregation: racial segregation. Ultimately, this means that school districts are strategically able to control both the demographics of students and the availability of resources. For example, school funding is connected directly to property tax. Hence, schools located in neighborhoods with more expensive homes will have greater funding than schools located in those with high concentrations of poverty. Now, let's examine this example a little deeper by looking at the connection between poverty and race. In 2019, the Children's Defense Fund reported that more than 70 percent of poor children in the United States are children of color. Moreover, in comparison to their white peers, Black children are three times as likely to grow up in poverty. This is important because no matter how much conservative, white educational leadership and policy makers desire to avoid the issue of race, an undeniable connection among poverty, race, and the dynamics of power and privilege remains. In fact, it is impossible to adequately address early childhood education reform for students of color without addressing race.

Michie (2012) declares that race must be positioned as a central theme in the process of school reformation, particularly in schools serving students of color. A color-blind approach, by contrast, would be a denial of the existence of institutional racism and systemic inequalities and a perpetuation of the social and cultural exclusion within education. This type of exclusion is reflected in the underrepresentation of children of color in gifted classrooms and their overrepresentation in suspensions and expulsions. Accordingly, Darling-Hammond (2005) emphasizes that systemic inequalities must be acknowledged before policies can be effective for all students. If they are not, these policies will continue to fail students of color by identifying them as the cause of their own failure. Thus, we as educators have to ensure that we make every effort to intentionally implement policies and practices that meet the needs of each and every child and family in our care and that we are willing to reassess and adjust when necessary. Although the previous example of school funding is beyond the immediate control of a single school or program, there are program- and classroom-specific issues that must be taken into consideration, including teaching and assessment practices and discipline policies. We discuss ways to advance equity in teaching and assessment in chapter 9. In this chapter, we highlight the immediate need to revise or create equitable discipline policies in our early education settings.

Working toward Equity in Discipline Policies

Many early childhood professionals are dismayed that preschoolers are suspended at three times the rate of K–12 students (Gilliam and Shahar, 2006). Children of color, and African American children in particular, are disproportionately impacted by preschool suspensions and expulsions. African American children make up 19 percent of preschool enrollment but represent 47 percent of preschoolers suspended one or more times (U.S. Department of Education, 2016). Factors such as challenging behaviors, lack of teacher training in culturally responsive instruction, and the cultural disconnect between school and home contribute to preschool suspension and expulsion (Derman-Sparks, LeeKeenan, and Nimmo, 2015; Perry et al., 2008; Ray, Bowman, and Robbins, 2006; Gilliam and Shahar, 2006). However, recent research suggests teachers' implicit racial bias is a contributing factor to the disproportionate rates at which African American children are suspended and expelled (Gilliam et al., 2016).

Examining and addressing implicit racial biases is a key factor in preventing preschool suspension and expulsion while strengthening teacher-child relationships. Center programs can create policies that avoid using suspensions as a first resort and can implement practices that eliminate disparate outcomes in disciplinary practices among African American children.

Although the governance of early childhood programs varies from state to state, U.S. states always have a preestablished set of behavior-management laws that licensed child-care facilities must follow in developing and implementing their discipline methods and practices. These laws typically mandate that practices be developmentally appropriate and must not incorporate any form of corporal punishment, physical discipline, or anything else that may cause children harm. Additionally, discipline cannot involve or be administered in relation to food, rest, or toileting. Although the laws are very clear and concrete about what discipline *cannot* be, they fail to set strict boundaries about what discipline *should* be, particularly as it relates to issues of expulsion and suspension. Unfortunately, although governing bodies are intentional in highlighting possible behavior-management strategies, such as redirection, ignoring minor misbehaviors, praising positive behaviors, allowing logical and natural consequences to occur, and even reserving time-out as a final resort, ambiguity remains about what characterizes misbehavior and whether removing a child from the learning environment completely is a viable ongoing strategy.

Consequently, interpretations of what behaviors qualify as either inappropriate or appropriate are at the subjective discretion of the program administrator. This means that a child's behavior is filtered through the administrator's personal beliefs and opinions about acceptable behavior, which are most likely rooted in their own cultural or internalized understandings. Hence, terms such as *noncompliance* and *disrespect* are used to justify disciplinary actions. It must be noted that these terms are typically measured according to normative white, middle-class behavior and leave very little room for cultural differences, which speaks to the disproportionate rates of suspensions and expulsions of African American students. There is often a clear contrast in perception of acceptable behaviors for ethnically diverse students and families and for those of their white, middle-class peers. This contrast is only exacerbated in school settings where students are expected to uphold a common code of conduct. For example, Hwa-Froelich and colleagues (2007) identify cultural differences in styles of politeness, with communication styles being commonly misunderstood and interpreted as evidence of conflict or poor social outcomes for minority students. Ethnically and culturally diverse students are often representative of high-context cultures, whose styles of communication typically contradict those required to thrive in the normative, low-context culture pervasive in education settings. In high-context cultures, nonverbal communication, such as facial expressions, tone of voice, and eye movement, is a primary method of conveying meaning during conversation. However, this type of communication is not only frowned upon in the classroom but is often misinterpreted as misbehaving, ultimately resulting in ethnically marginalized students being punished for simply being authentically themselves.

Darling-Hammond (2005) insists that before policies can be effective for all students, systematic inequalities must be acknowledged. Otherwise, policies will continue to fail minority students by identifying them as the cause of their failure. Townsend (2000) notes the importance of structuring rules in schools to foster positive learning environments for all students rather than forcing all students to adopt the cultural values and beliefs of white, middle-class culture. Arbitrary rules that focus more on socializing ethnically and culturally diverse students into white middle-class culture only perpetuate the cultural divide between the groups and prevent fairly distributed disciplinary actions. Rules must be evaluated according to whether they are essential to creating nurturing, safe learning environments for all students. It is for this reason that early education programs must develop discipline policies and practices that do not depend on exclusion. These policies and practices must explicitly outline strategies for addressing the role of implicit bias and cultural differences in the misinterpretation of behavior.

Strategies to Prevent Preschool Suspensions

The following are some strategies that we suggest every early childhood program include in their discipline policies and practices to ensure that the programs are equitable for each and every child.

Reflecting on Biases

Early childhood educators need opportunities to reflect on their biases and discuss what they uncover. Taking the Implicit Bias Association Test is a great way for teachers to examine and reflect on their biases. The Implicit Bias Association test, created by Harvard University, is a tool to help individuals uncover unconscious beliefs they may have. The test, available at https://implicit.harvard.edu/implicit/takeatest.html, is designed to measure attitudes and beliefs that people may be unwilling or unable to report (Office for Equity, Diversity, Inclusion, and Belonging, Harvard University, 2022).

Examining these biases allows educators to reflect on children's behavior that may have triggered various negative responses. After reflecting, teachers need a safe space to engage in conversations about their biases. Talking openly and honestly about biases not only helps people understand where our biases come from but also allows teachers to challenge their biases and change those automatic reactions. Let's look at a few examples.

Biased Thoughts	Strengths-Based Thoughts
"That mom always comes to the school in pajama pants and a bonnet to drop the child off."	"The mom is always eager to volunteer in the classroom."
"That child's hair is never combed when she comes to school."	"The grandmother ensures the child is at school on time and does a wonderful job helping her transition into the school environment."
"He doesn't know English that well."	"The child is becoming bilingual."

Having Honest Discussions

Talking about biases is a good first step. However, engaging in honest conversations about anti-Blackness, race, and racism is equally important. *Anti-Blackness* is a form of racism that devalues Blackness and systematically marginalizes Black people. Because African American people have been maligned across the globe and narratives that African American people are inherently inferior are deeply rooted in society and American institutions, it can be challenging to unpack all the ways anti-Blackness shows up in the classroom, in play, in the curriculum, and in lesson planning, but it is imperative to do so if we want to create equitable learning environments. Educators, particularly white educators, often struggle with talking about race and racism; however, having open, honest discussions about race has been shown to reduce some of the implicit biases that influence racial inequity in schools (Skiba et al., 2011). Talking about race allows teachers to have authentic relationships with children and families of color.

Consider some ways administrators, teachers, and other school staff can begin having honest conversations about race. For example, reviewing data on the disparities in rates of suspensions and expulsions among preschool

African American children is an excellent way to introduce conversations about race and racial biases. Watching documentaries such as the following can open up authentic conversations about race and develop a deeper understanding of the history of racism in America.

✦ *I Am Not Your Negro* (2016) written by James Baldwin; directed by Raoul Peck

✦ *13th* (2016) written by Spencer Averick and Ava DuVernay; directed by Ava DuVernay

✦ *The African Americans: Many Rivers to Cross* (2013) written by Henry Louis Gates, Jr., and Donald Yacovone; directed by Sabin Streeter (episodes 1 and 2), Jamila Wignot (episodes 3 and 6), Phil Bertelsen (episodes 4 and 5), and Leslie Asako Gladsjo (episode 6)

✦ *Who We Are: A Chronicle of Racism in America* (2021) written by Emily Kunstler and Sarah Kunstler; directed by Jeffery Robinson

✦ *Civil: Ben Crump* (2022) directed by Nadia Hallgren

While the following book list is not an exhaustive one, any of these books is a good starting point for having authentic, open, and honest conversations about race in America.

Alexander, Michelle. 2010. *The New Jim Crow: Mass Incarceration in the Age of Colorblindness.* New York: The New Press.

Anderson, Carol. 2016. *White Rage: The Unspoken Truth of Our Racial Divide.* New York: Bloomsbury.

DiAngelo, Robin. 2018. *White Fragility: Why It's So Hard for White People to Talk about Racism.* Boston, MA: Beacon Press.

DiAngelo, Robin. 2022. *Nice Racism: How Progressive White People Perpetuate Racial Harm.* Boston, MA: Beacon Press.

Hall, Thomas D., and James V. Fenelon. 2016. *Indigenous Peoples and Globalization: Resistance and Revitalization.* London, UK: Routledge.

Kendi, Ibram X. 2019. *How to Be an Antiracist.* New York: One World.

Oluo, Ijeoma. 2019. *So, You Want to Talk about Race.* New York: Seal Press.

Rothstein, Richard. 2018. *The Color of Law: A Forgotten History of How Our Government Segregated America.* New York: Liveright Publishing.

Saad, Layla F. 2020. *Me and White Supremacy: Combat Racism, Change the World, and Become a Good Ancestor.* Naperville, IL: Sourcebooks.

Building Authentic Relationships with Families

In their study on implicit biases and preschool suspension, Walter Gilliam and colleagues (2016) found that children are less likely to be suspended when teachers have relationships with their families. Research shows that children perform better when families are engaged in their children's education. Building authentic partnerships with families allows teachers and center directors to gain a deeper understanding of family dynamics, acquire insight about the family's cultural background, and make meaningful connections.

Creating Culturally Responsive Classrooms

Geneva Gay, Gloria Ladson-Billings, and Carol Brunson Day have written and spoken extensively on the need to create culturally responsive classrooms. Creating culturally responsive classrooms goes beyond including diverse children's books in the classroom or displaying children of color on a bulletin board. While those efforts are needed, culturally responsive classrooms ensure that the children's cultural references are intentionally included in the overall learning environment. For example, in the dramatic play area, teachers can include dolls with different skin tones and hair textures from various ethnic backgrounds, ethnic play food and cooking utensils such as tortilla presses and woks, and clothing such as head wraps, scarves, sandals, and moccasins. These items demonstrate to children that their culture is not only represented in the classroom but is also valued. Teachers can ask families for suggestions about what type of cultural artifacts are appropriate to include in the classroom. This ensures that teachers are not inadvertently perpetuating stereotypical items.

Another critical component of creating a culturally responsive classroom is helping build a positive racial and ethnic identity for young children. Too often, children of color internalize negative messages about their racial or ethnic group that they see on television, read or see in books, receive in their neighborhoods, or even experience in their schools. Helping children take pride in their cultural backgrounds and in themselves helps build their self-esteem and increase their self-efficacy.

Creating culturally responsive classrooms requires teachers to create an environment where all students are welcomed, supported, and provided with the best opportunities to learn, regardless of their cultural and linguistic backgrounds (Barnes, 2006). Culturally responsive education is an approach that includes a student's unique cultural heritage in learning to promote academic achievement (Ladson-Billings, 1998). In practice, a culturally responsive classroom should:

✦ encourage positive racial and ethnic identity development,

✦ prevent exclusion and isolation,

✦ recognize the accomplishments and contributions of people of color, and

✦ incorporate the student's culture into the learning environment.

Following are a few ideas teachers can implement to help build children's positive racial and ethnic identity.

Work with Families to Support Social-Emotional Needs

Because behavior is a form of communication, early childhood programs in partnership with families can develop plans based on principles of trauma-informed care to meet the social-emotional needs of children.

✦ **Safety:** Throughout the program and classroom, children need to feel physically and psychologically safe.

✦ **Trust and transparency:** Decisions about children's learning and development are made in partnership with the family to demonstrate trust, transparency, and respect for the family's goals for their child's education.

✦ **Collaboration:** Differences in power are acknowledged and addressed in an effort to create an environment that promotes shared decision-making between families and school personnel.

With all of this in mind, educators still may not know how to incorporate these ideals into a practicable plan when addressing specific issues that students are dealing with. The following is a sample plan for working with a family to address an issue occurring in the classroom and at home.

PLAN TO MEET CHILD'S SOCIAL AND EMOTIONAL NEEDS

Child's name: Mya Harris   **Date:** January 28, 2022

Adults present: Teacher: Ms. Paige; Family Members: Mom and Stepfather; Director: Ms. Kelly

Child behavior: Swearing at home and at school

Background information: Mom had a baby with her new husband 8 weeks ago. Mya remained in the center during the maternity leave. Swearing began the week the baby brother started attending the center. Mya's dad transferred to another state for work and hasn't visited in 3 months.

Child's possible emotions: Mya seems to display a range of emotions before and after swearing. We have seen amusement, sadness, boredom, and frustration.

Contextual cues: We notice that Mya seems to look around at others before and after swearing, as if to gauge their reactions. She laughs at the reactions. She is by herself and appears bored before she swears.

Possible unmet social needs: attention?

Plan to meet need(s):

✦ **Environments:** Move Mya's cot to the front of the room, closer to the teacher, so it's easier for the teacher to rub her back and see the rest of the room.

✦ **Experiences:** Allow Mya to help with snack time for the week.

- Find time to let Mya pick a story for the literacy circle.
- Give Mya a turn in the reader chair.
- Help Mya write letters to her father.

✦ **Relationships:** Once a week, Mom will spend 5 minutes in the classroom with Mya.

- Read notes to Mya from Mom when sent in.
- Once a week, arrange for mom to call Mya at school.
- Mom and stepfather will look for opportunities to spend one-on-one time with Mya.

✦ **Outside resources:** None at this time

✦ **Follow-up date:** Weekly phone calls as needed

Source: Salcedo, Michelle. 2018. *Uncover the Roots of Challenging Behaviors: Create Responsive Environments Where Young Children Can Thrive.* Minneapolis, MN: Free Spirit.

In the plan, we see the embedded principles of safety, trust, transparency, and collaboration. Mya's cot will be moved closer to the teacher so the teacher can rub Mya's back when she is feeling unsafe or needs a little extra attention. Trust and collaboration are demonstrated in the relationship column through the activities that the family and teacher cocreated to help Mya feel more secure and receive the attention she needs.

Attend Racial-Equity Training

Teachers and directors need ongoing professional development and coaching to change practices and behaviors. Attending a racial-equity training is important as early childhood classrooms become more culturally and linguistically diverse. Racial equity involves identifying and eliminating the practices and policies that produce inequitable outcomes for children. However, it should be noted that attending one racial-equity training session is not enough. Racial-equity work is not about checking a box; it is an intentional investment that happens over time. When teachers and center directors prioritize racial equity, they create anti-racist learning environments.

These strategies can set the tone for addressing implicit racial bias. As early childhood educators are responsible for the well-being of the whole child, including their academic, health, social-emotional, and cognitive development, there is an ethical duty and responsibility to ensure all children have equitable treatment in schools. It is illogical to suspend children from the very environments that were designed to support their social-emotional and academic growth. Early childhood educators have a responsibility to ensure young children have equal and equitable access to high-quality early learning experiences that provide instruction that meets the unique learning needs regardless of a child's racial and ethnic background, socioeconomic status, language skill, or ability.

REFLECTING ON EQUITABLE POLICIES AND PRACTICES

✦ What are some of the assumptions, biases, and prejudices you may hold about children and their families? Create a list and think about where your biases about the group came from.

✦ Next, write down ways you can challenge your biases.

✦ How can you lead and teach for equity in the face of implicit bias?

✦ What are some ways you can create a more culturally responsive and welcoming classroom?

CHAPTER 9

Next Steps: Cultivating the Identities, Agency, and Voices of Racially and Ethnically Diverse Learners

Ebonyse's Experience

"I have been teaching for forty years, and I was trained not to see color. I have been carrying around this color-blind notion for all these years thinking I was doing something wonderful by not seeing the color of my students' skin, and what I was really doing was ignoring race and their racial identity."

This quote is from one of the participants I interviewed as I conducted research for my dissertation. As this teacher mentioned, she was trained not to see a child's skin color. For forty years, she ignored the racial and cultural identities of the children in her care. She thought a color-blind ideology was a best practice to engage with racially and ethnically diverse children.

This teacher is not alone. Most early childhood teachers are trained to embrace a color-blind approach. As I (Ebonyse) interviewed early childhood teachers for my dissertation to learn how their teacher education program prepared them to educate and engage with culturally diverse students, many of the teachers reported they were taught to not see the color of a child, rather to see the child as an individual. While the intent of a color-blind approach is to treat all children equally, this approach ignores the issues of race and institutional biases in education and prevents teachers from seeing children as members of their racial and cultural groups (Wardle, 2007; York, 2016).

Talking about Race

Race plays a significant role in how we view ourselves as racial beings. So much of who we are is shaped by our racial and ethnic identity. Most people identify with their racial group. In fact, Omi and Winant (2014) argue that without a racial identity, one is in danger of having no identity at all. Children's racial and ethnic culture shape how they see themselves in the world and greatly influence their sense of self, identity, and self-efficacy.

Because race is central to our identity, it is imperative for educators and administrators to understand the impact race and racism has on children's development. Research shows that preschool children not only recognize race but also develop racial biases as early as age three (Aboud, 2005). Adults often believe that preschool children are too young to discuss race or that mentioning race to children is somehow divisive (Winkler, 2009).

Talking about race with children is not divisive in a society where race plays a role in children's outcomes.

Children of color and Black children in particular are fully aware of race-based discrimination. In the film *Reflecting on Anti-Bias Education in Action: The Early Years* (McKinney, 2021), one of the teachers discusses her reaction when a Black preschool boy asked her if she knew that George Floyd was killed by a white police officer and whether he, too, would be killed because he was Black. At the tender age of five, no child should be concerned with whether they will be killed by a police officer because of their skin color. However, the reality is that African American children understand racial discrimination early on. They understand the concept of being treated differently based on skin color. Because preschool children recognize race and develop racial biases, and young African American children and other children of color internalize racist messages and experience discrimination based on race, teachers need to have authentic, developmentally appropriate conversations about race in the classroom. Having these conversations about race and racism in a developmentally appropriate way helps children make sense of the world around them and teaches them to become anti-racist advocates.

Following are a few strategies that teachers can employ when discussing race with young children:

✦ Let children know it's okay to acknowledge and embrace racial differences.

✦ Examine your own racial biases and challenge them when triggered.

✦ In the overall learning environment, discuss and incorporate the contributions of people of color to the United States (and not just during Black History Month).

✦ Answer children's questions honestly. If you don't know the answer to something they ask, say that and tell the child you will follow up. (Then, of course, actually follow up.)

✦ Avoid getting defensive or exhibiting negative facial expressions when children ask questions. Instead, respond with, "I am really glad you asked me that question. Let's talk about it."

✦ Push through your discomfort. Sit with your discomfort and seek to understand why you are uncomfortable. Find a friend who will hold you accountable for continuing to do critical self-reflection.

✦ Create lesson plans that expose children to different cultural opportunities, and discuss the experiences afterward.

Building a Positive Racial and Ethnic Identity in Children

Ebonyse's Experience

Discussing race with young children can help build and affirm a positive racial and ethnic identity. In my home when I was growing up, the teaching of racial pride and celebrating Black culture was commonplace. My father was adamant about helping me build a positive self-concept and racial identity. When I was nine years old, my father explained to me that the ancient Egyptians were Black people. He stated that they were highly intelligent and built great civilizations in Africa. He noted that the word Egypt came from the name the Greeks had given

*their land: Aigyptos. The word Kemet, meaning "Black land,"
was what the Egyptians called their home. As he talked about
the Egyptians, my father said firmly, "Do not let anyone ever tell
you they were not Black people." My nine-year-old brain did not
know how to conceptualize this information, but what I could
understand was the seriousness of his tone, so I listened intently.*

*Lessons about Africa were coupled with acknowledging
Black excellence and celebrating cultural holidays such as
Kwanzaa and Juneteenth. My father made certain I knew
the contributions of Black people throughout history who
fought for Black liberation. While Dr. Martin Luther King, Jr., is
renowned, loved, and celebrated in many African American
families, people such as Malcolm X, Marcus Garvey, Toussaint
Louverture, Fannie Lou Hamer, Ida B. Wells, Fred Hampton,
Angela Davis, Stokely Carmichael (Kwame Ture), and Nat Turner
were the heroes who were celebrated in our home. My father
felt it was important to know the contributions of these African
Americans because they demonstrated Black unity, racial
pride, and concepts that promoted a positive racial identity.
These individuals fought for Black liberation through means
of self-determination and economic self-sufficiency. Stories of
economically thriving Black communities such as Black Wall
Street in Tulsa, Oklahoma, were examples of not only Black
liberation but also racial pride.*

*Our celebration of Kwanzaa demonstrated a way to connect
to African traditions while also affirming African family and
social values. The seven principles of Kwanzaa serve as a guide
to help build and reinforce unity among the African diaspora.
Similarly, celebrating Juneteenth not only represents freedom
but promotes knowledge and appreciation of African American
history, and it fosters a sense of community as well. Having these
experiences as part of my socialization as a young child were
crucial in developing a positive sense of self and racial identity.*

Research suggests that families who discuss race and racism with their
preschool-age children can positively affect their children's well-being.
Caughy, O'Campo, and Muntaner (2004) found that when African American

parents actively confront issues of racism, they report lower rates of anxiety and depression in their preschool-aged children. Similarly, Nash and colleagues (2018) conducted ethnographic studies to further understand how children are racially socialized overtime. One of the authors conducted mini lessons about Africa with her granddaughters. These lessons included discussions about the meaning of African symbols, looking at a map of Africa, reading children's literature and watching movies that take place in Africa, and learning that Africa is the beginning of civilization (Nash et al., 2018). It is important for young Black children to learn their history before slavery, because this gives them a sense of pride and achievement about African contributions to world history.

Creating Anti-Racist Early Childhood Programs

Early childhood programs could learn lessons from African American families to build positive racial identities for young African Americans and other children of color. Racial socialization is critical in developing the social and emotional well-being of young racially and ethnically diverse children. Teachers can play a pivotal role in the development of identity, self-esteem, beliefs, and positive attitudes about their race in African American children and other children of color. However, teachers must become comfortable discussing race and racism by doing the self-work first. This includes reading books, attending webinars, engaging in difficult conversations, watching documentaries, reflecting on the information learned, and having continued conversations to process and unpack the new information.

Second, teachers must acknowledge and challenge their implicit racial biases. Taking the Implicit Bias Association test will help teachers become aware of the biases they hold and reflect on ways to challenge them. The Kirwan Institute for the Study of Race and Ethnicity has a four-part online training module on implicit bias. Teachers can dive deeper into understanding implicit biases, including understanding the origins of biases and ways to actively challenge them. One way for teachers and administrators to intentionally challenge their implicit biases is to look for the strengths of each child. Instead of focusing on what the child is lacking or how the child is "misbehaving," consider the strengths the child has. For example, if a child constantly talks during story time, consider making the child the story helper for the day. The child can help the teacher read certain words or turn the pages of the book.

Next, teachers can adopt anti-racist perspectives and pedagogy. Adopting anti-racist perspectives requires teachers not only to acknowledge the racial hierarchy in our society and the consequences racism has on the lives of people of color, but also to understand that the American educational system was founded on historically racist practices. In practice, adopting an anti-racist pedagogy goes beyond teachers acknowledging the cultural and linguistic diversity in their classroom. Rather, it entails:

✦ examining the historical roots of racism and understanding the implications racial discrimination has on children's academic success;

✦ actively challenging policies, practices, and attitudes that routinely produce racial inequities in educational settings;

✦ including the contributions of African Americans and other people of color into the curriculum;

✦ reconciling the hypocrisy around some American values, such as justice for all and equal treatment under the law;

✦ challenging the dominant European worldview and incorporating more inclusive perspectives from marginalized and oppressed groups;

✦ refraining from teaching a whitewashed curriculum and instead telling an accurate version of American history (for example, not teaching that Christopher Columbus "discovered" America); and

✦ teaching intentionally with a critical and equitable lens that disrupts systems of oppression, power, and privilege.

It is imperative for educators to understand that because we have all been socialized in a racist society, adopting an anti-racist pedagogy is not just good for African American children and other children of color; it is good for all children. As our early childhood classrooms become increasingly diverse, educators must get comfortable discussing race and racism, and they must learn how to affirm and build positive racial identities for children of color. As professionals entrusted with the care of young children, we have a responsibility to promote racial equity in early childhood. All children have a right to learn in an environment where their identity is affirmed, celebrated, and respected.

DIVING DEEPER

These resources will further your understanding of young children and race and discussing race with young children:

Learning for Justice. https://www.learningforjustice.org/

Mead, Ebonyse. 2021. "Being Mindful of the Unintended Consequences of Having the Talk with My Black Male Child." *Journal of Curriculum and Pedagogy* 19(3): 278–280. https://www.tandfonline.com/eprint/A84VFJPFSNZBKAIW3JMC/full?target=10.1080/15505170.2021.1912861

Netflix Jr. 2020. *Common Reads "Let's Talk About Race."* Bookmarks series. Video. https://www.youtube.com/watch?v=40ORHCOA9fE

PBS Kids. 2020. *Talk About: Race and Racism*. Video. https://youtu.be/_fbQBKwdWPg

PBS Kids. 2021. *Talk About: Race, Racism, and Identity*. Video. https://youtu.be/B5moq6_5LSk

Queensland Department of Education. 2016. *Embedding Culture in Practice*. Video. https://www.youtube.com/watch?v=SJ_Ra8MnFe8

WNYC. 2015. *Because I'm Latino, I Can't Have Money? Kids on Race.* Video. https://www.youtube.com/watch?v=C6xSyRJqIe8

Woke Kindergarten. https://www.wokekindergarten.org/

These children's books can be used to foster positive discussions of race with children in the classroom:

Leung, Christine T. 2021. *What I See: Anti-Asian Racism from the Eyes of a Child*. LegaC Publishing.

Maillard, Keith N. 2019. *Fry Bread: A Native American Family Story.* New York: Roaring Brook Press.

Pinkney, Sandra L. 2006. *Shades of Black: A Celebration of Our Children*. New York: Scholastic.

Pinkney, Sandra L. 2007. *I Am Latino: The Beauty in Me*. New York: Little, Brown Books for Young Readers.

REFERENCES AND RECOMMENDED READING

Aboud, Frances E. 2005. "The Development of Prejudice in Childhood and Adolescence." In *On the Nature of Prejudice: Fifty Years after Allport*. Malden, MA: Blackwell.

Akua, Chike. 2020. "Standards of Afrocentric Education for School Leaders and Teachers." *Journal of Black Studies* 51(2): 107.

Alexander, Michelle. 2012. *The New Jim Crow: Mass Incarceration in the Age of Colorblindness*. New York: The New Press.

Allen, Ayana, Lakia M. Scott, and Chance W. Lewis. 2013. "Racial Microaggressions and African American and Hispanic Students in Urban High Schools: A Call for Culturally Affirming Education." *Interdisciplinary Journal of Teaching and Learning* 3(2): 117–129.

Allen, Sarah, Diane Duncan Perrote, and Saul Feinman. 2022. "Family Life Education with Indigenous Families." In *Family Life Education with Diverse Populations*. Thousand Oaks, CA: SAGE.

Bakadorova, Olga, and Diana Raufelder. 2017. "The Interplay of Students' School Engagement, School Self-Concept, and Motivational Relations during Adolescence." *Frontiers in Psychology* 8: 2171. doi: 10.3389/fpsyg.2017.02171

Banks, James A., and Cherry A. M. Banks, eds. 2001. *Multicultural Education: Issues and Perspectives*. 4th ed. Boston, MA: Allyn and Bacon.

Barnes, Charline J. 2006. "Preparing Preservice Teachers to Teach in a Culturally Responsive Way." *The Negro Educational Review* 57(1–2): 85–100.

Baugh, Eboni J., and DeAnna R. Coughlin. 2012. "Family Life Education with Black families." In *Family Life Education with Diverse Populations*. Thousand Oaks, CA: SAGE.

Beeman, Angie. 2015. "Walk the Walk, but Don't Talk the Talk: The Strategic Use of Colorblind Ideology in an Interracial Social Movement Organization." *Sociological Forum* 30(1): 127–147.

Berk, Laura E., and Adena B. Meyers. 2016. *Infants, Children, and Adolescents*. 8th ed. Boston, MA: Pearson Education.

Bonilla-Silva, Eduardo. 2018. *Racism without Racists: Colorblind Racism and the Persistence of Racial Inequality in America*. 5th ed. Lanham, MD: Rowman and Littlefield.

Boutte, Gloria S. 2012. "Urban Schools: Challenges and Possibilities of Early Childhood and Elementary Education." *Urban Education* 47(2): 515–550.

Boutte, Gloria S., Julia Lopez Robertson, and Elizabeth Powers-Costello. 2011. "Moving Beyond Colorblindness in Early Childhood Classrooms." *Early Childhood Education Journal* 39(5): 339–342.

Boutte, Gloria. S., & Jennifer Strickland. (2008). "Making African American culture and history central to early childhood teaching and learning." *The Journal of Negro Education*, 77(2), 131-142.

Boykin, W. Alfred. 1994. "Afrocultural Expression and Its Implications for Schooling." In *Teaching Diverse Populations: Formulating a Knowledge Base*. Albany, NY: State University of New York Press.

Boykin, W. Alfred, and Forrest D. Toms. 1985. "Black Child Socialization: A Conceptual Framework." In *Black Children: Social, Educational, and Parental Environments*. Beverly Hills, CA: SAGE.

Bredekamp, Sue. 2019. *Effective Practices in Early Childhood Education: Building a Foundation*. Upper Saddle River, NJ: Pearson Education.

Bronson, Jennifer, and Ann Carson. 2019. *Prisoners in 2017*. Washington, DC: Office of Justice Programs, U.S. Bureau of Justice Statistics, U.S. Department of Justice. https://bjs.ojp.gov/content/pub/pdf/p17.pdf

Brophy, Jere. 2008. "Developing Students' Appreciation for What Is Taught in Schools." *Educational Psychologist* 43(3): 132–141.

Brown v. Board of Education of Topeka. 347 U.S. 483 (1954).

Bryk, Anthony S., and Barbara Schneider. 2003. "Trust in Schools: A Core Resource for School Reform." *Educational Leadership* 60(6): 40–44.

Calzada, Esther J., et al. 2015. "Family and Teacher Characteristics as Predictors of Parent Involvement in Education during Early Childhood among Afro-Caribbean and Latino Immigrant Families." *Urban Education* 50(7): 870–896.

Caughy, Margaret O., Saundra M. Nettles, Patricia J. O'Campo, and Kimberly F. Lohrfink. 2006. "Neighborhood Matters: Racial Socialization of African American Children." *Child Development* 77(5): 1220–1236.

Caughy, Margaret O., Patricia J. O'Campo, and Carles Muntaner. 2004. "Experiences of Racism among African American Parents and the Mental Health of Their Preschool-Aged Children." *American Journal of Public Health* 94(12): 2118–2124.

Cherng, Hua-Yu S. 2016. "Is All Classroom Conduct Equal? Teacher Contact with Parents of Racial/Ethnic Minority and Immigrant Adolescents." *Teachers College Record* 118(11): 1–32.

Child Trends. 2018. "Racial and Ethnic Compositions of the Child Population: Indicators of Child and Youth Well-Being."Child Trends. https://www. childtrends.org/www.childtrends.org/?indicators=racial-and-ethnic-composition-of-the-child-population

Children's Defense Fund. 2021. "Child Poverty." *The State of America's Children 2021.* Washington, DC: Children's Defense Fund. https://www. childrensdefense.org/wp-content/uploads/2021/04/The-State-of-Americas-Children-2021.pdf

Christie, Michael, Michael Carey, Ann Robertson, and Peter Grainger. 2015. "Putting Transformative Learning Theory into Practice." *Australian Journal of Adult Learning* 55(1): 9–30.

Counts, Jennifer, Antonis Katsiyannis, and Denise K. Whitford. 2018. "Culturally and Linguistically Diverse Learners in Special Education: English Learners." *NASSP Bulletin* 102(1): 5–21.

Corr, Allison, and Josh Wenderoff. 2022. "Inequitable Access to Oral Care Continues to Harm Children of Color: Analysis of Outcomes among Third-Graders Highlights Gaps in Data." Pew Charitable Trusts. https://www. pewtrusts.org/en/research-and-analysis/articles/2022/03/11/inequitable-access-to-oral-health-care-continues-to-harm-children-of-color

Cox, Barbara, and Manuel Ramirez III. 1981. "Cognitive Styles: Implications for Multiethnic Education." In *Education in the 80's: Multiethnic Education.* Washington, DC: National Education Association.

Cranton, P. (2016). *Understanding and promoting transformative learning: A guide to theory and practice.* San Francisco CA: Jossey-Bass.

Crawford, Gisele M., and Oscar A. Barbarin. 2006. "Acknowledging and Reducing the Stigmatization of African American Boys." *Young Children* 61(6): 79–85.

Civil Rights Project/Proyecto Derechos Civiles. 2010. "K–12 Education." The Civil Rights Project. https://civilrightsproject.ucla.edu/research/k-12-education/

Darling-Hammond, Linda. 2005. "New Standards and Old Inequalities: School Reform and the Education of African American Students." In *Black Education: A Transformative Research and Action Agenda for the New Century.* New York: Routledge.

Dasgupta, Nilanjana. 2004. "Implicit Ingroup Favoritism, Outgroup Favoritism, and Their Behavioral Manifestations." *Social Justice Research* 17(2): 143–168.

Dasgupta, Nilanjana. 2013. "Implicit Attitudes and Beliefs Adapt to Situations: A Decade of Research on the Malleability of Implicit Prejudices,

Stereotypes, and the Self-Concept." *Advances in Experimental Social Psychology* 47: 233–279.

Davis, F. James. 1991. *Who Is Black? One Nation's Definition.* University Park, PA: Pennsylvania State University Press.

Davis, Bonnie M. 2007. *How to Teach Students Who Don't Look Like You: Culturally Relevant Teaching Strategies.* Thousand Oaks, CA: Corwin Press.

DeGruy, Joy. 2017. *Post Traumatic Slave Syndrome: America's Legacy of Enduring Injury and Healing.* Revised ed. Portland, OR: Joy DeGruy Publications.

Delgado, Richard, and Jean Stefancic. 2012. *Critical Race Theory: An Introduction.* 2nd ed. New York: New York University Press.

Derman-Sparks, Louise, and Julie Olsen Edwards. 2010. *Anti-Bias Education for Young Children and Ourselves.* Washington, DC: National Association for the Education of Young Children.

Derman-Sparks, Louise, Debbie LeeKeenan, and John Nimmo. 2015. *Leading Anti-Bias Early Childhood Programs: A Guide for Change.* Washington, DC: National Association for the Education of Young Children.

Dixson, Adrienne D., and Celia K. Rousseau, eds. 2006. *Critical Race Theory in Education: All God's Children Got a Song.* New York: Taylor and Francis Group.

Doucet, Fabienne, Meeta Banerjee, and Stephanie Parade. 2016. "What Should Young Black Children Know about Race? Parents of Preschoolers, Preparation for Bias, and Promoting Egalitarianism." *Journal of Early Childhood Research* 16(1): 1–15.

Dunham, Yarrow, Andrew S. Baron, and Mahzarin R. Banaji. 2008. "The Development of Implicit Intergroup Cognition." *Trends in Cognitive Sciences* 12(7): 248–253.

Dunn, Rita, Shirley Griggs, and Gary E. Price. 1993. "Learning Styles of Mexican American and Anglo-American Elementary-School Students." *Journal of Multicultural Counseling and Development* 21(4): 237-247.

DuVernay, Ava, director. 2016. *13th.* Netflix. Film. 1 hr., 40 mins.

Ely, Danielle, M., and Anne K. Driscoll. 2021. "Infant Mortality in the United States, 2019: Data from the Period Linked Birth/Infant Death File." *National Vital Statistics Reports* 70(14). https://www.cdc.gov/nchs/data/nvsr/nvsr70/nvsr70-14.pdf

English, Devin, et al. 2020. "Daily Multidimensional Racial Discrimination among Black U.S. American Adolescents." *Journal of Applied Developmental Psychology* 66(Jan.–Feb.): 101068.

Evans-Winters, Venus E. 2011. *Teaching Black Girls: Resiliency in Urban Classrooms.* Revised ed. New York: Peter Lang.

Ewing, Norma J., and Fung L. Yong. 1992. "A Comparative Study of the Learning-Style Preferences among Gifted African-American, Mexican-American and American-Born Chinese Middle Grade Students." *Roeper Review* 14(3): 120–123.

Fabelo, Tony, et al. 2011. *Breaking Schools' Rules: A Statewide Study of How School Discipline Relates to Students' Success and Juvenile Justice Involvement.* New York: Council of State Governments Justice Center.

Fantuzzo, John, Christine McWayne, Marlo A. Perry, and Stephanie Childs. 2004. "Multiple Dimensions of Family Involvement and Their Relations to Behavioral and Learning Competencies for Urban, Low-Income Children." *School Psychology Review* 33(4): 467–480.

Ferguson, Harvey B., Sarah Bovaird, and M. P. Mueller. 2007. "The Impact of Poverty on Educational Outcomes for Children." *Paediatrics and Child Health* 12(8): 701–706.

Friedman, Norman L. 1967. "Cultural Deprivation: A Commentary in the Sociology of Knowledge." *The Journal of Educational Thought* 1(2): 88–99.

Gay, Geneva. 2010. *Culturally Responsive Teaching: Theory, Research, and Practice.* 2nd ed. New York: Teachers College Press.

Gay, Geneva, and Tyrone C. Howard. 2001. "Multicultural Teacher Education for the 21st Century." *The Teacher Educator* 36(1): 1–16.

Gibson, Priscilla A., et al. 2014. "The Role of Race in the Out-of-School Suspensions of Black Students: The Perspectives of Students with Suspensions, Their Parents, and Educators." *Children and Youth Services Review* 47(3): 274–282.

Gillanders, Cristina, Marvin McKinney, and Sharon Ritchie. 2012. "What Kind of School Would You Like for Your Children: Exploring Minority Mothers' Beliefs to Promote Home-School Partnerships." *Journal of Early Childhood Education* 40(5): 285–294.

Gilliam, Walter S., et al. 2016. *Do Early Educators' Implicit Biases Regarding Sex and Race Relate to Behavior Expectations and Recommendations of Preschool Expulsion and Suspensions?* Research study brief. New Haven, CT: Yale Child Study Center. https://medicine.yale.edu/childstudy/zigler/publications/Preschool%20Implicit%20Bias%20Policy%20Brief_final_9_26_276766_5379_v1.pdf

Gilliam, Walter S., and Golan Shahar. 2006. "Preschool and Child Care Expulsion and Suspension: Rates and Predictors in One State." *Infants and Young Children* 19(3): 228–245.

Gitanjali, Saluja, Diane M. Early, and Richard M. Clifford. 2002. "Demographic Characteristics of Early Childhood Teachers and Structural Elements of Early Care in the United States." *Early Childhood Research and Practice* 4(1).

Goff, Phillip Atiba, et al. 2014. "The Essence of Innocence: Consequences of Dehumanizing Black Children." *Journal of Personality and Social Psychology* 106(4): 526–545.

Golash-Boza, Tonya. 2016. "A Critical and Comprehensive Sociological Theory of Race and Racism." *Sociology of Race and Ethnicity* (2)2: 129–141.

Graham, Sandra, and Brian S. Lowery. 2004. "Priming Unconscious Racial Stereotypes about Adolescent Offenders." *Law and Human Behavior* 28(5): 483–504.

Grant, Kathy B. and Julie A. Ray. 2013. *Home, School, and Community Collaboration: Culturally Responsive Family Engagement.* 2nd ed. Thousand Oaks, CA: SAGE.

Greenwald, Anthony G., Debbie E. McGhee, and Jordan L. K. Schwartz. 1998. "Measuring Individual Differences in Implicit Cognition: The Implicit Association Test." *Journal of Personality and Social Psychology* 74(6): 1464–1480.

Gregory, Anne, and Pharmicia M. Mosely. 2004. "The Discipline Gap: Teachers' Views on the Over-Representation of African American Students in the Discipline System." *Equity and Excellence in Education* 37(1): 18–30.

Gregory, Anne, Russell J. Skiba, and Pedro A. Noguera. 2010. "The Achievement Gap and the Discipline Gap: Two Sides of the Same Coin?" *Educational Researcher* 39(1): 59–68.

Grier, William H., and Price M. Cobbs. 1968/1992. *Black Rage: Two Black Psychiatrists Reveal the Full Dimensions of the Inner Conflicts and the Desperation of Black Life in the United States.* New York: Basic Books.

Griggs, Shirley, and Rita Dunn. 1996. "Hispanic-American Students and Learning Style." ERIC Digest. https://files.eric.ed.gov/fulltext/ED393607.pdf

Gross, Samuel R., Maurice Possley, and Klara Stephens. 2017. *Race and Wrongful Convictions in the United States.* Irvine, CA: National Registry of Exonerations, Newkirk Center for Science and Society, University of California Irvine. https://www.law.umich.edu/special/exoneration/Documents/Race_and_Wrongful_Convictions.pdf

Hale, Janice E. 1986. *Black Children: Their Roots, Culture and Learning Styles*. Revised ed. Baltimore, MD: The Johns Hopkins University Press.

Hale, Janice E. 2016. "Learning Styles of African American Children: Instructional Implications." *Journal of Curriculum and Teaching* 5(2): 109–118.

Harry, Beth, and Janette Klingner. 2006. *Why Are So Many Minority Students in Special Education? Understanding Race and Disability in Schools*. New York: Teachers College Press.

Harvard T. H. Chan School of Public Health. 2016. "Health Disparities between Blacks and Whites Run Deep." Harvard T. H. Chan School of Public Health. https://www.hsph.harvard.edu/news/hsph-in-the-news/health-disparities-between-blacks-and-whites-run-deep/

Hawley, Willis D., and Sonia Nieto. 2010. "Another Inconvenient Truth: Race and Ethnicity Matter." *Educational Leadership* 68(3): 66–71.

Hemmings, Carrie, and Amanda M. Evans. 2018. "Identifying and Treating Race-Based Trauma in Counseling." *Journal of Multicultural Counseling and Development* 46(1): 20–39.

Hilliard, Asa G. 1976. *Alternatives to IQ Testing: An Approach to the Identification of Gifted "Minority" Children*. Report. Sacramento, CA: California State Board of Education. https://files.eric.ed.gov/fulltext/ED147009.pdf

Hilliard, Asa G. 1989. "Teachers and Cultural Styles in Pluralistic Society." NEA Today 7(6): 65–69.

Hinchey, Patricia H. 2010. *Finding Freedom in the Classroom: A Practical Introduction to Critical Theory*. Revised ed. New York: Peter Lang Publishing.

Hollins, Etta, and Maria Torres Guzman. 2005. "Research on Preparing Teachers for Diverse Populations." In *Studying Teacher Education: The Report of the AERA Panel on Research and Teacher Education*. Mahwah, NJ: Lawrence Erlbaum.

hooks, bell. 1994. *Teaching to Transgress: Education as the Practice of Freedom*. London, UK: Routledge.

Howard, Tyrone C. 2018. "Capitalizing on Culture: Engaging Young Learners in Diverse Classrooms." *Young Children* 73(2): 24-33.

Howes, Carollee, et al. 2008. "Ready to Learn? Children's Pre-Academic Achievement in Pre-Kindergarten Programs." *Early Childhood Research Quarterly* 23(1): 27–50.

Hunter, Margaret. 2005. *Race, gender, and the politics of skin tone.* New York: Routledge.

Husband, Terry. 2019. "Using Multicultural Picture Books to Promote Racial Justice in Urban Early Childhood Literacy Classrooms." *Urban Education* 54(8): 1058–1084.

Hwa-Froelich, Deborah, Danai C. Kasambira, and Amy Marie Moleski. 2007. "Communicative Functions of African American Head Start Children." *Communication Disorders Quarterly* 28(2): 77–91.

Hwang, Shann Hwa (Abraham). 2012. "Family Life Education with Asian Immigrant Families." In *Family Life Education with Diverse Populations.* Thousand Oaks, CA: SAGE.

Hwang, Shann Hwa (Abraham). 2022. "Family Life Education with Asian Immigrant Families." In *Family Life Education with Diverse Populations.* 2nd ed. San Diego, CA: Cognella Academic Publishing.

Irvine, Jacqueline J. 2003. *Educating Teachers for Diversity: Seeing with a Cultural Eye.* New York: Teachers College Press.

Irving B. Harris Foundation. n.d. "Diversity-Informed Tenets for Work with Infants, Children, and Families." The Tenets. https://diversityinformedtenets.org/the-tenets/english/

Ishimaru, Ann M. 2019. "From Family Engagement to Equitable Collaboration." *Educational Policy* 33(2): 350–385.

Jalali, Fatemeh A. 1988. "A Cross-Cultural Comparative Analysis of the Learning Styles and Field Dependent/Independence Characteristics of Selected Fourth-, Fifth-, and Sixth-Grade Students of Afro, Chinese, Greek, and Mexican Heritage." Doctoral diss. Jamaica, NY: St. John's University.

Janzen, Bonnie, et al. 2017. "Racial Discrimination and depression among On-Reserve First Nations People in Rural Saskatchewan." *Canadian Journal of Public Health* 108(5–6): e482–e487.

Jarret, Robin L., and Sarai Coba-Rodriguez. 2015. "'My Mother Didn't Play about Education': Low-Income, African American Mothers' Early School Experiences and Their Impact on School Involvement for Preschoolers Transitioning to Kindergarten." *Journal of Negro Education* 84(3): 457–472.

Jean-Sigur, Raynice, Douglas Bell, and Yanghee Kim. 2015. "Building Global Awareness in Early Childhood Teacher Preparation Programs." *Childhood Education* 92(1): 3–9.

King, Martin Luther, Jr. 1963. "I Have a Dream." Washington, DC, August 28. NPR. https://www.npr.org/2010/01/18/122701268/i-have-a-dream-speech-in-its-entirety

Kinney, Aaron. 2005. "'Looting' or 'Finding'?" Salon. https://www.salon.com/2005/09/02/photo_controversy/

Kubota, Ryuko, and Angel M. Y. Lin, eds. 2009. *Race, Culture, and Identities in Second Language Education: Exploring Critically Engaged Practice*. New York: Routledge.

Kunjufu, Jawanza. 2002. *Black Students. Middle Class Teachers*. Chicago, IL: African American Images.

Ladson-Billings, Gloria. 1998. "Just What Is Critical Race Theory and What's It Doing in a *Nice* Field Like Education?" *International Journal of Qualitative Studies in Education* 11(1): 7–24.

Ladson-Billings, Gloria. 2009. *The Dreamkeepers: Successful Teachers of African American Children*. 2nd ed. San Francisco, CA: Jossey-Bass.

Legette, Kamiliah B., Leoandra O. Rogers, and Chezare A. Warren. 2020. "Humanizing Student-Teacher Relationships for Black Children: Implications for Teachers' Social-Emotional Training." *Urban Education* 57(2): 278–288.

Lesane-Brown, Chase L. 2006. "A Review of Race Socialization within Black Families." *Developmental Review* 26(4): 400–426.

Lewis, Amanda, E., and John B. Diamond. 2015. *Despite the Best Intentions: How Racial Inequality Thrives in Good Schools*. New York: Oxford Press.

Loomis, Alysse M. 2021. "The Influence of Early Adversity on Self-Regulation and Student-Teacher Relationships in Preschool." *Early Childhood Research Quarterly* 54(1): 294–306.

Losen, Daniel J., and Tia Elena Martinez. 2013. *Out of School and Off Track: The Overuse of Suspensions in American Middle and High Schools*. Los Angeles: The UCLA Center for Civil Rights Remedies at the Civil Rights Project. https://files.eric.ed.gov/fulltext/ED541735.pdf

Losen, Daniel J., and Russell J. Skiba. 2010. "Suspended Education: Urban Middle Schools in Crisis." The Civil Rights Project. http://civilrightsproject.ucla.edu/research/k-12-education/ school-discipline/suspended-education-urban-middle-schools-in-crisis

Marin, Jennifer R., et al. 2021. "Racial and Ethnic Differences in Emergency Department Diagnostic Imaging at US Children's Hospitals, 2016–2019." *JAMA Network Open* 4(1): e2033710. doi:10.1001/jamanetworkopen.2020.33710

McIntosh, Kent, Erik J. Girvan, Robert H. Horner, and Keith Smolkowski. 2015. "Education not Incarceration: A Conceptual Model for Reducing Racial and Ethnic Disproportionality in School Discipline." *Journal of Applied Research on Children: Informing Policy for Children at Risk* 5(2): 1–22.

McKinney, Filiz Efe, director. 2021. *Reflecting on Anti-Bias Education in Action: The Early Years.* Film. 48 mins. Anti-Bias Leaders in Early Childhood Education. https://www.antibiasleadersece.com/the-film-reflecting-on-anti-bias-education-in-action/

McWayne, Christine M., et al. 2013. "Defining Family Engagement among Latino Head Start Parents: A Mixed-Methods Measurement Development Study." *Early Childhood Research Quarterly* 28(3): 593–607.

Mead, Ebonyse. 2021. "Being Mindful of the Unintended Consequences of Having the Talk with My Black Male Child." *Journal of Curriculum and Pedagogy* 19(3): 278–280.

Meece, Darrell, and Kimberly O. Wingate. 2009. "Providing Early Childhood Teachers with Opportunities to Understand Diversity and the Achievement Gap." *SRATE Journal* 19(1): 36–43.

Merck, Amanda. 2020. "Report: 1 in 5 U.S. Latino, Black Children Have Obesity." Salud America! https://salud-america.org/report-1-in-5-u-s-latino-black-children-have-obesity/#:~:text=One%20of%20five%20children%20of%20color%20have%20obesity.,%2839.8%25%29%20children%20as%20compared%20to%20white%20children%20%2811.7%25%29

Michie, Gregory. 2012. *We Don't Need Another Hero: Struggle, Hope, and Possibility in the Age of High-Stakes Schooling.* New York: Teachers College Press.

Milner, H. Richard, IV. 2006. "The Promise of Black Teachers' Success with Black Students. *Educational Foundations* 20 (3–4): 89–104.

Milner, H. Richard, IV. 2013. "Analyzing Poverty, Learning, and Teaching through a Critical Race Theory Lens." *Review of Research in Education* 37(1): 1–53.

Minami, Masahiko, and Carlos J. Ovando. 2004. "Language Issues in Multicultural Contexts." In *Handbook of Research on Multicultural Education.* 2nd ed. San Francisco, CA: Jossey-Bass.

Morgan, Hani. 2009. "What Every Teacher Needs to Know to Teach Native American Students." *Multicultural Education* 16(4): 10–12.

Morrison, George, Mary J. Woika, and Lorraine Breffni. 2020. *Fundamentals of Early Childhood Education.* 9th ed. Upper Saddle River, NJ: Pearson Education.

Morrison, George, S. 2008. *Early Childhood Education Today* (11th edition). Upper Saddle River, NJ: Prentice Hall.

Nash, Kindel, et al. 2018. "Critical Racial Literacy in Homes, Schools, and Communities: Propositions for Early Childhood Contexts." *Contemporary Issues in Early Childhood* 19(4): 1–18.

National Association for the Education of Young Children. 2019. *Advancing Equity in Early Childhood Education.* Position statement. https://www.naeyc.org/resources/position-statements/equity

National Center for Education Statistics. 2013. "Table 209.10. Number and Percentage Distribution of Teachers in Public and Private Elementary and Secondary Schools, by Selected Teacher Characteristics: Selected Years, 1987–88 through 2011–12." Digest of Education Statistics. https://nces.ed.gov/programs/digest/d13/tables/dt13_209.10.asp

National Low Income Housing Coalition. 2019. "Racial Disparities among Extremely Low-Income Renters." National Low Income Housing Coalition. https://nlihc.org/resource/racial-disparities-among-extremely-low-income-renters#:~:text=Twenty%20percent%20of%20black%20households%2C%2018%25%20of%20American,homeownership%20rates%20and%20higher%20incomes%20among%20white%20households

Nellis, Ashley. 2021. "The Color of Justice: Racial and Ethnic Disparity in State Prisons." The Sentencing Project. https://www.sentencingproject.org/publications/color-of-justice-racial-and-ethnic-disparity-in-state-prisons/

Neville, Helen A., Miguel E. Gallardo, and Derald Wing Sue, eds. 2016. *The Myth of Racial Colorblindness: Manifestations, Dynamics, and Impact.* Washington, DC: American Psychological Association.

Noguera, Pedro A. 2008. "Introduction: Part III: City Classrooms, City Schools." In *City Kids, City Schools: More Reports from the Front Row.* New York: New Press.

Nores, Milagros, and Steven W. Barnett. 2014. *Access to High Quality Early Care and Education: Readiness and Opportunity Gaps in America.* CEELO Policy Report. New Brunswick, NJ: Center on Enhancing Early Learning Outcomes.

Nutton, Jennifer, and Elizabeth Fast. 2015. "Historical Trauma, Substance Use, and Indigenous Peoples: Seven Generations of Harm from a 'Big Event.'" *Substance Use and Misuse* 50(7): 839–847.

O'Connor, Carla, and Sonia DeLuca-Fernandez. 2006. "Race, Class, and Disproportionality: Reevaluating the Relationship between Poverty and Special Education Placement." *Educational Research* 35(6): 6–11.

Office for Equity, Diversity, Inclusion, and Belonging, Harvard University. 2022. "Where Everyone Can Thrive." Office for Equity, Diversity, Inclusion, and Belonging. https://edib.harvard.edu/

Okonofua, Jason A., and Jennifer L. Eberhardt. 2015. "Two Strikes: Race and the Disciplining of Young Students." *Psychological Sciences* 26(5): 617–624.

Omi, Michael, and Howard Winant. 2015. *Racial Formation in the United States*. 3rd ed. New York: Routledge.

Orosco, Michael J., and Janette Klingner. 2010. "One School's Implementation of RTI with English Language Learners: 'Referring into RTI.'" *Journal of Learning Disabilities* 43(3): 269–288.

Osai, Keith, V. and Jacob Fitisemanu. 2022. "Family Life Education with Native Hawaiian and Pacific Islander American Families." In *Family Life Education with Diverse Populations*. 2nd ed. San Diego, CA: Cognella Academic Publishing.

Patten, Eileen, 2016. Racial, gender wage gaps persist in U.S. despite some progress. Pew Research Center. https://www.pewresearch.org/fact-tank/2016/07/01/racial-gender-wage-gaps-persist-in-u-s-despite-some-progress/

Peck, Raoul, director. 2016. *I Am Not Your Negro*. Amazon Studios. 1 hr., 35 mins.

Perry, Deborah F., M. Clare Dunne, LaTanya McFadden, and Doreen Campbell. 2008. "Reducing the Risk for Preschool Expulsion: Mental Health Consultation for Young Children with Challenging Behaviors." *Journal of Child and Family Studies* 17(1): 44–54.

Pewewardy, Cornel. 2002. "Learning Styles of American Indian/Alaska Native Students: A Review of Literature and Implications for Practice." *Journal of American Indian Education* 41(3): 22–56.

Pewewardy, Cornel. 2008. "Learning styles of American Indian/Alaska Native Students. In *Classic Edition Sources: Multicultural Education*. New York: McGraw-Hill.

Pinto, Erica. 2010. *The Unequal Opportunity Race*. Film. African American Policy Forum. https://www.youtube.com/watch?v=vX_Vzl-r8NY

Pfeiffer, J. William. 1993. *The 1993 Annual, Developing Human Resources*. San Diego, CA: Pfeiffer & Co.

Race Forward. n.d. "What Is Racial Equity?" Race Forward. https://www.raceforward.org/about/what-is-racial-equity-key-concepts

Ray, Aisha, Barbara Bowman, and Jean Robbins. 2006. *Preparing Early Childhood Teachers to Successfully Educate All Children: The Contribution of Four-Year Undergraduate Teacher Preparation Programs.* Chicago, IL: Erikson Institute. https://www.fcd-us.org/assets/2016/04/TeacherPreparationPrograms.pdf

Robinson, Jeffery, director. 2021. *Who We Are: A Chronicle of Racism in America.* Film. Sony Pictures. 1 hr., 57 mins.

Roediger, David, R. 1991. *The wages of whiteness.* New York: Verso .

Rothstein, Richard. 2017. *The Color of Law: A Forgotten History of How Our Government Segregated America.* New York: Liveright Publishing.

Salcedo, Michelle. 2018. *Uncover the Roots of Challenging Behavior: Create Responsive Environments Where Young Children Thrive.* Minneapolis, MN: Free Spirit Publishing.

Schofield, Janet W. 2010. "The Colorblind Perspective in School: Causes and Consequences." In *Multicultural Education: Issues and Perspectives.* 7th ed. New York: John Wiley and Sons.

Schvaneveldt, Paul. 2022. "Family Life Education with Latino/Latina Immigrant Families." In *Family Life Education with Diverse Populations.* 2nd ed. San Diego, CA: Cognella Academic Publishing.

Schvaneveldt, Paul, and Andrew O. Behnke. 2012. "Family Life Education with Latino Immigrant Families." In *Family Life Education with Diverse Populations.* Thousand Oaks, CA: SAGE.

Seaton, Eleanor K. 2010. "The Influence of Cognitive Development and Perceived Racial Discrimination on the Psychological Well-Being of African American Youth." *Journal of Youth and Adolescence* 39(6): 694–703.

Sensoy, Özlem, and Robin DiAngelo. 2017. *Is Everyone Really Equal? Key Concepts in Social Justice Education.* 2nd ed. New York: Teachers College Press.

Shade, Barbara J. 1989. "The Influence of Perceptual Development on Cognitive Style: Cross Ethnic Comparisons." *Early Childhood Development and Care* 51(1): 137–155.

Sims, J. 1988. "Learning Styles of Black-American, Mexican-American, and White-American Third- and Fourth-Grade Students in Traditional Public Schools." Doctoral diss. Santa Barbara, CA: University of California at Santa Barbara.

Singham, Mano. 1998. "The Canary in the Mine: The Achievement Gap between Black and White Students." *Phi Delta Kappan* 80(1): 8–15.

Skiba, Russell J., et al. 2011. "Race Is Not Neutral: A National Investigation of African American and Latino Disproportionality in School Discipline." *School Psychology Review* 40(1): 85–107.

Snyder, Thomas D., Cristobal de Brey, and Sally A. Dillow. 2018. *Digest of Education Statistics 2016*. Washington, DC: National Center for Education Statistics. https://nces.ed.gov/pubs2017/2017094.pdf

Souto-Manning, Mariana. 2013. *Multicultural Teaching in the Early Childhood Classroom: Approaches, Strategies and Tools, Preschool–2nd Grade*. New York: Teachers College Press and Washington, DC: Association for Childhood Education International.

Staats, Cheryl. 2015. "Understanding Implicit Bias: What Educators Should Know." *American Educator* 39(4): 29–33.

Staats, Cheryl, and Charles Patton. 2013. *State of the Science: Implicit Bias Review 2013*. Columbus, OH: Kirwan Institute for the Study of Race and Ethnicity, The Ohio State University.

Statman-Weil, Katie. 2020. *Trauma-Responsive Strategies for Early Childhood*. St. Paul, MN: Redleaf Press.

Steele, Claude M., and Joshua Aronson. 1995. "Stereotype Threat and the Intellectual Test Performance of African Americans." *Journal of Personality and Social Psychology* 69(5): 797–811.

Stevenson, Howard C. 2013. *If Elephants Could Talk: Healing Racial Stress in Schools*. New York: Teachers College Press.

Streeter, Sabin, et al. 2013. *The African Americans: Many Rivers to Cross*. Film. PBS. 6 hrs.

Sullivan, Amanda L. 2011. "Disproportionality in Special Education Identification and Placement of English Language Learners." *Exceptional Children* 77(3): 317–334.

Sullivan, Debra R. 2016. *Cultivating the Genius of Black Children: Strategies to Close the Achievement Gap in the Early Years*. St. Paul, MN: Redleaf Press.

Swisher, Karen G. 1991. "American Indian/Alaska Native Learning Styles: Research and Practice." ERIC Digest. Washington, DC: Office of Educational Research and Improvement.

Teranishi, Robert T. 2015. "Asian Pacific Americans and Critical Race Theory: An Examination of School Racial Climate." *Equity and Excellence in Education* 35(2): 144–154.

Terrell, Francis, and Sandra L. Terrell. 1981. "An Inventory to Measure Cultural Mistrust among Blacks." *The Western Journal of Black Studies* 5(3): 180–184.

Terrell, Francis, Sandra L. Terrell, and Fayneese Miller. 1993. "Level of Cultural Mistrust as a Function of Educational and Occupational Expectations among Black Students." *Adolescence* 28(111): 593–596.

Terrill, Marguerite M., and Dianne L. H. Mark. 2000. "Preservice Teachers' Expectations for Schools with Children of Color and Second-Language Learners." *Journal of Teacher Education* 51(2): 149–55.

Thomas, Deja, and Richard Fry. 2020. "Prior to COVID-19, Child Poverty Rates Had Reached Record Lows in the U.S." Pew Research Center. https://www.pewresearch.org/fact-tank/2020/11/30/prior-to-covid-19-child-poverty-rates-had-reached-record-lows-in-u-s/

Tileston, Donna W. 2010. *What Every Teacher Should Know about Diverse Learners*. 2nd ed. Thousand Oaks, CA: Corwin.

Tobin, Tary J., and Claudia G. Vincent. 2011. "Strategies for Preventing Disproportionate Exclusions of African American Students." *Preventing School Failure* 55(4): 192–201.

Townsend, Brenda L. 2000. "The Disproportionate Discipline of African American Learners: Reducing School Suspensions and Expulsions." *Exceptional Children* 66(3): 381–391.

Trang, Kim T., and David M. Hansen. 2021. "The Roles of Teacher Expectations and School Composition on Teacher-Child Relationship Quality." *Journal of Teacher Education* 72(2): 152–167.

Ukpokodu, Nelly. 2002. "Breaking through Preservice Teachers' Defensive Dispositions in a Multicultural Education Course: A Reflective Practice." *Multicultural Education* 9(3): 25–33.

USA Facts. 2020. "White People Own 86% of Wealth and Make up 60% of the Population." USA Facts. https://usafacts.org/articles/white-people-own-86-wealth-despite-making-60-population/

U.S. Government Accountability Office. 2020. "Racial Disparities in Education and the Role of Government." U.S. Government Accountability Office. https://www.gao.gov/blog/racial-disparities-education-and-role-government

U.S. Department of Education Office for Civil Rights. 2016. *A First Look: Key Data Highlights on Equity and Opportunity Gaps in Our Nation's Public Schools*. Washington, DC: U.S. Department of Education. https://files.eric.ed.gov/fulltext/ED577234.pdf

U.S. Department of Education Office of Civil Rights. 2014. *Civil Rights Data Collection: Data Snapshot: School Discipline.* Issue Brief no. 1. Washington, DC: U.S. Department of Education. https://ocrdata.ed.gov/assets/downloads/CRDC-School-Discipline-Snapshot.pdf

U.S. Department of Health and Human Services, Administration for Children and Families, Office of Head Start, National Center on Parent, Family, and Community Engagement. 2018. *Head Start Parent, Family, and Community Engagement Framework.* 2nd ed. https://eclkc.ohs.acf.hhs.gov/sites/default/files/pdf/pfce-framework.pdf

Vasquez, J.A. 1991. "Cognitive Style and Academic Achievement." In *Cultural Diversity and the Schools: Consensus and Controversy.* London, UK: Falconer Press.

Waites, Cheryl. 2009. "Building on Strengths: Intergenerational Practice with African American Families." *Social Work* 54(3): 278–287.

Wardle, Francis. 2007. "Multiracial Children in Child Development Textbooks." *Early Childhood Education Journal* 35(3): 253–259.

Wardle, Francis. 2018. "Adding to Our View of Early Childhood Multicultural Education." *Childhood Education* 94(5): 34–40.

Watkins, Angela F. 2002. "Learning Styles of African American Children: A Developmental Consideration." *Journal of Black Psychology* 28(1): 3–17.

Wenger, Etienne, Richard McDermott, and William Snyder. 2002. *Cultivating Communities of Practice: A Guide to Managing Knowledge.* Boston, MA: Harvard Business School Press.

White, Aisha, and Shannon B. Wanless. 2019. "P.R.I.D.E.: Positive Racial Identity Development in Early Education." *Journal of Curriculum, Teaching, Learning, and Leadership in Education* 4(2): Article 9.

Wildenger, Leah K., and Laura L. McIntyre. 2011. "Family Concerns and Involvement during Kindergarten Transition." *Journal of Child and Family Studies* 20(4): 387–396.

Willis, Madge G. 1989. "Learning Styles of African American Children: A Review of the Literature and Interventions." *Journal of Black Psychology* 16(1): 47–65.

Winkler, Erin N. 2009. "Children Are Not Colorblind: How Young Children Learn Race." *PACE* 3(3): 1–8.

York, Stacey. 2016. *Roots and Wings: Affirming Culture in Early Childhood Programs.* St. Paul, MN: Redleaf Press.

INDEX

A

Acculturation, 7, 58

Acknowledging privilege, 43

Activities to promote racial pride, 66

Administrators, 4–5, 50, 87, 90–91

African American students, 115–116

    culture of communalism, 3, 53–55, 57–58

    higher suspension rates, 1, 4–5, 12, 18, 25–26, 40

    preferred learning styles, 57–58

Allocating resources, 43

Analytical thinking style, 53

Anti-Blackness, 3–4, 7, 108–110

Asian American students

    filial piety, 54

    high-context culture, 55

Assessment practices, 2–3

Assimilation, 7, 58

Authentic relationships, 5–7, 38–47, 67–82, 110

B

Barriers to engaging diverse families, 39–41

Behavior management strategies, 105–106

Black codes, 15

Black cultural experience, 71

Black History Month, 116

Black Wall Street (Tulsa, Okla.), 117

Brown v. Board of Education of Topeka, 11–12, 103–104

C

Children's books, 4, 93, 120

Children's Defense Fund, 13, 104

Cognitive engagement, 58

Collaborative learning, 57

"Color-blind" approach, 5, 18–22, 70–74, 114–115

Colorism, 61

Community of practice, 31–37

Cooperative learning, 56, 59

Creating anti-racist programs, 118–120

Critical race theory, 7, 22–23

Cultural audits, 45

Cultural autobiography, 76–77

Cultural awareness, 48–52

Cultural deprivation theory, 21

Cultural disconnect, 2–5, 18–29, 39

Cultural identity, 2–3, 48–66

    African American students, 57–58

    characteristics of European-American, 53

    comparison of high- and low-context cultures, 55

    cultural iceberg model, 50–52

    importance of equitable learning environments, 59–65

    Latine students, 58–59

    Native American students, 49

    racial socialization, 65–66

    social location, 49–50

Cultural-deficit model, 39–41

Culturally responsive anti-bias (CRAB) education, 3, 5, 30–37

    learning in a community of practice, 31–37

    vs. traditional, 28

Culturally responsive environments, 110–113

Culturally sustainable instructional practices, 5, 82–102

    equity advisory board, 89

    establishing a plan, 82–83

    preparing the learning environment, 91–96

    taking action, 96–102

Culture, 7, 30–31, 48, 52–55, 83–85, 106

D

Deep culture, 50–51

Deficit ideology, 75

Distorting dilemma, 32–33

Diversity-informed tenets, 5, 42–44

Documentaries to help talk about race, 14, 109, 115, 120

"Doll Study" (Clark & Clark), 61, 63

E

Early childhood educators, 4–5

    authentic relationships with children, 67–81

    reflecting on assumptions about children, 69

    establishing, 69–70

    social awareness, 70–72

    putting social awareness into practice, 72–74

    reflecting on bias, 72

    self-awareness, 74–76

    putting self-awareness into practice, 76

    implicit bias tests, 77

    instructional accountability, 77–80

    reflecting on the needs of diverse learning, 80

    putting instructional accountability into action, 80–1

    reflecting on instructional accountability, 81

    creating anti-racist programs, 118–120

    mostly white, non-Hispanic, monolingual, and middle class, 3, 19

    reflecting on social location, 50

Emotional engagement, 58

Engaged pedagogy, 78–80

Equitable learning environments, 59–65

Equity advisory board, 89

Equity/anti-bias checklist, 81

Ethnicity, 2–3, 7

European-American culture, 52–55

Examining program practices and policies, 6, 103–113

Experiential learning, 57

F

Families

    "all about our family" survey, 86

    family treasure chest, 86

    building authentic relationships with, 38–47

    barriers to engaging with, 39–41

    new strategies for, 41–44

    strategies to promote inclusivity, 44–47

    sharing in decision-making, 4

    traditional methods of engaging, 5

    culturally responsive engagement, 5

    check-ins, 73

    getting to know, 72, 83–85

    promoting engagement, 94–96

    putting engagement into practice, 95–

    town halls, 95

    surveys, 95

    leadership, 95–96

    engagement projects, 96

    building authentic relationships with, 110

    working with to support children's social-emotional needs, 111–113

Familismo, 54

Field-dependent learners, 59

G

Gifted and talented programs, 12

H

Habit building, 89–91

Hawaiian/Pacific Islander students

    culture of family interdependence, 54

    high-context culture, 55

Head Start, 18, 42, 95–96, 98

High vs. low-context cultures, 55

Historical trauma, 5, 8, 15–17

I

Immigrant families, 2–3

Immigration status, 58

Implicit bias tests, 76, 107, 118

Implicit bias, 3, 5, 8, 17–18, 23–27, 39–40, 74–77

Inclusivity, 41, 44–46, 110–111

Indigenous students. *See* Native American students

Individualism, 53–54

Institutional racism, 3, 5, 8, 10–17

Instructional accountability, 77–81
engaged pedagogy, 78–80
reflecting on the needs of diverse learners, 80
putting into action, 80–81
reflective journaling, 80
professional learning communities, 80–81
difficult conversations, 81
equity/anti-bias checklist, 81
reflecting on, 81

Intergenerational trauma. *See* Historical trauma

J

Juneteenth, 117

K

Kinesthetic learning, 3, 58–59

KWL charts, 79–80

L

Latine children
discipline disparities, 11
culture of family interdependence, 54
preferred learning styles, 58–59
several unique cultures, 58
high-context culture, 55

Learning environment. *See* Preparing the learning environment

Learning for Justice, 120

Learning styles. *See* Preferred learning styles

M

Maintaining the program, 89–91

Mass incarceration, 14–15

Meritocracy, 5, 18, 20, 22–23

Microaggressions, 8, 65

"Model minority" groups, 60

Multicultural education, 20–21

N

Native American students
historical trauma, 15–17
culture of family interdependence, 54
high-context culture, 55
preferred learning styles, 56

Negative media images, 23–24, 64–65

O

Overidentification, 61

P

Parent-teacher conferences, 38

Pathologizing family practices, 38–39

Pathologizing young children, 21

Pay disparities, 12–13

Peer learning, 5, 31, 36–37, 59

Planning, 82–83, 112

Post-traumatic slave syndrome (PTSS), 8, 16

Poverty, 2–3, 12–13, 104

Preferred learning styles, 3, 5
cultural preferences, 52, 55–59
Native American students, 56
African American students, 57–58
Latine students, 58–59

Preparing the learning environment, 91–96
displays, toys, and instructional materials, 91–93
professional development, 93–94
promoting family engagement, 94–96

Professional development, 3, 73–74, 93–94, 113

Professional learning communities, 80–81

Project Implicit, 77

R

Race, 2–3, 8

Racial identity, 115–117

Racial literacy, 75–76

Racial socialization, 65–66, 118–120

Racism, 8, 115–116

Redlining, 11

Respect, 41, 43–44, 85

S

Safety, 31, 91, 111

School discipline policies

working toward equity in, 104–108

reflecting on our own experiences
in school, 107

strategies to prevent
preschool suspensions, 108–110

implicit bias and, 25–27

disparities, 6, 11, 40

Segregated schools, 103–104

Self–awareness, 43, 74–77

Self-reflection, 5, 34–36, 78,
80, 83–89, 107–108

Self-responsibility/self-sufficiency, 53–54

Social awareness, 70–74

Social justice, 22

Social learning theory (Bandura), 56

Social location, 49–50, 84

Socialization, 9

Special education, 18, 40

Spirituality, 57

Stereotype threat, 9, 59–60, 66

Stereotypes, 3, 59

in children's books, 4, 93

social awareness, 70–74

Strategies for family engagement, 41–44

Strategies to prevent
preschool suspensions, 107–110

reflecting on bias, 107–108

having honest conversations, 108–110

documentaries to help
with conversations, 109

books to help
with conversations, 109–110

buiilding relationships
with families, 110

Strategies to promote inclusivity, 44–46

cultural audits, 45

home visits, 45

cultural nights, 45

attending
neighborhood events, 45–46

hosting school events in
the community, 45–46

reflecting on, 46

Strengths-based approach, 86

Student achievement, 3–17

Superiority, 63–64

Surface culture, 50–51

T

Talking about race, 6

books to help talk with children, 120

books to help with, 109–110

building a positive racial and ethnic
identity in children, 116–118

difficult conversations, 39, 81, 108–110

documentaries to help with, 109, 115

with children, 6, 114–116

with families, 73

Transformative learning theory, 5, 32–36

Transportation barriers, 46

Trust, 85, 111

U

Unconscious culture, 51–52

Understanding the power
of language, 43–44

W

White superiority, 10

Whiteness, 3–4, 9

Woke Kindergarten, 120